SEASONS OF A FAMILY'S LIFE

Cultivating the Contemplative Spirit at Home

Wendy M. Wright
Foreword by Robert Benson

JOSSEY-BASS
A Wiley Imprint
www.josseybass.com

Library of Congress Cataloging-in-Publication Data
Wright, Wendy M.
Seasons of a family's life: cultivating the contemplative spirit at home /
Wendy M. Wright; foreword by Robert Benson.
p. cm.—(The families and faith series)
Includes bibliographical references.
ISBN 0-7879-5579-5 (alk. paper)
1. Family—Religious life. 2. Spiritual life—Christianity. I. Title. II. Series.
BV4526.3 .W75 2003
248.4—dc21
2002014794

Printed in the United States of America
FIRST EDITION
HB Printing   10 9 8 7 6 5 4 3 2 1

THE FAMILIES AND FAITH SERIES

The Families and Faith Series is devoted to exploring the relationship between the spiritual life and our closest human relationships. From one generation to the next, faith and families are deeply intertwined in powerful ways. Faith puts all of life, including family life, in such a large perspective that it invites the gratitude, wonder, and hope so badly needed in the middle of the complexities and struggles of existence. On the other hand, faith becomes real only as it lives through concrete human relationships. Religion needs families and communities where the generations gather together and share and celebrate what it means to love God and to love others. At their best, faith and families are immersed in grace, and this series hopes to be a resource for those seeking to make love real in their families, congregations, and communities.

Diana R. Garland

> Director, Baylor Center for Family and Community Ministry
> Baylor University

J. Bradley Wigger

> Director, Center for Congregations and Family Ministries
> Louisville Presbyterian Theological Seminary

SERIES EDITORS

TITLES IN THE FAMILIES AND FAITH SERIES
Sacred Stories of Ordinary Families: Living the Faith in Daily Life
> Diana R. Garland
Let the Children Come: Reimagining Childhood from a Christian Perspective
> Bonnie J. Miller-McLemore
The Power of God at Home: Nurturing our Children in Love and Grace
> J. Bradley Wigger
Seasons of a Family's Life: Cultivating the Contemplative Spirit at Home
> Wendy M. Wright

CONTENTS

FOREWORD

This is what I first remember about Wendy Wright.

She was standing in front of a crowd of sixty or so of us, a crowd of seekers and pilgrims and would-be contemplatives who were trying to learn something about the ancient ways of contemplative prayer and how to transpose those things into our late twentieth-century, anglo-saxon, protestant, middle-class ways of living. She was teaching us about the liturgical calendar of the church.

"Christmas," she said, "is the season in which we rise up on tiptoes to dance."

I wrote it down, unnecessarily as it turns out. It was written permanently somewhere inside me in that place where the language of the head and the language of the heart meet to form the language of the spirit.

There are those of us who are drawn to the contemplative life—a listening awareness that allows the Word to take root in the heart and transform it, as Wendy Wright herself describes in these pages. We are seeking some ground of connection between the Silence that is at the center of all things and the hustle and bustle of the lives that we actually lead.

We spend a fair portion of our lives reading books and going on retreats and otherwise trying to learn about and attempt to practice the ancient traditions of prayer and devotion to which we are drawn. We wonder from time to time if we are not called to be apart from the world in some way, to live in silence and contemplation, somewhere serene and quiet. We spend the other part of our lives facing up to and living in and out of the realities and pressures that are part and parcel of life in our time and our place, in our work and our homes.

It seems to me sometimes that those of us who share this sensibility and who have families have an especially difficult time. The sheer pace, the number of hours, the other sorts of demands that make up a life with children make it seem as though quiet and silence and stillness—the sort of things that give rise to the contemplative life—are generally impossible to come by.

Fortunately, for those us who have wandered into her classes or her workshops or the retreats that she directs or the books that she writes, Wendy Wright stands with us.

In the first place, she simply knows an extraordinary amount about the ancient traditions and practices and history of the life of prayer that is the contemplative Christian tradition. When she writes about ritual and pilgrimage and formation, when she writes about contemplation and discernment and community, she knows what she is talking about. Such knowledge is the fruit of a life spent—as a student, as a pilgrim, as a teacher—following the call of those ancient ways on her own heart. And she is perceptive and gifted when it comes to describing and explaining those ancient practices to the rest of us in ways that connect them to the kind of lives that we lead.

Which is a good reason to listen to her, but not the only one.

When she writes she tells her own stories, the stories of her own family and her own joys and her own struggles. And she tells them with honesty and clarity and grace. When she writes about forgiveness and mercy and gratitude, she writes as a witness, without sentimentality and without preaching. When she tells those stories, you can see them. Better still, you can see your own stories more clearly, and can begin to see how the contemplative life is—and can be— more a part of your life than you had hoped possible.

For those of us who seek the contemplative life in the midst of ordinary life, Wendy Wright is a treasure. She knows whereof she speaks, and she speaks the truth.

And, perhaps best of all, she is a poet. She writes sentences that you remember about the things that really matter. Which is why I wanted to rise up on my tiptoes and dance when I read this book.

Nashville, Tennessee   Robert Benson
November 2002

PREFACE

More than anything else I have written, this book—*Seasons of a Family's Life*—has emerged out of who I *am,* in contrast to what I do or what I know. I am a professional academician, a historian of Christian spirituality who teaches this tradition to students at universities and in pastoral settings. I do this as a practicing Roman Catholic who is deeply involved in both ecumenical formation and interfaith dialogue.

I am also a wife and a mother. My husband and I have three young-adult children—two girls and a boy. It has been the amazing, often painful, often ecstatic adventure of being a parent that has most *formed* me—to use the traditional Christian term usually reserved for the training of priests or persons in vowed religious life. It is parenting that has made, unmade, and remade me into someone who comes up hard against the great religious questions that have always been part of the human quest: Who in fact *am* I? What *is* a life well led? What is most essential, permanent, and foundational? What responsibility do I have to others? How do I deal with evil and fear? What is "the good"? How do I love well? How do I move in this wild and worrisome world with some grace and joy?

This is not the first time I have written about being a parent. My first book on family spirituality was *Sacred Dwelling: A Spirituality of Family Life.* The approach of that book was to take the ordinary experiences of family life and, through the ancient spiritual practice of attentiveness, to allow the presence of sacred reality to emerge—in other words, to see what is really there. In *Sacred*

Dwelling, I used the spatial device of walking through the rooms of a home to discover the dynamics of family life intrinsic to each particular space. Further, I used my knowledge of the spiritual traditions of Christianity to illuminate family dynamics. The weaving together of contemporary experience and ancient tradition was never one-sided. Experience was enriched by tradition, but tradition was sometimes reinterpreted, critiqued, and reassessed. *Seasons of a Family's Life* also represents a dialogue between classic spiritual tradition and experience in the home. It also grew out of necessity. I needed to write this book for myself and for our children as a record of the way they have made me who I am.

I wrote *Sacred Dwelling* when my children were between the ages of two and ten, both of my parents were alive, and most of the elder generation of my husband's family was living. In the intervening years, our children have grown and we are nearly empty-nested. My husband's and my place in the family has also changed dramatically. Both my father and my mother-in-law have died, as has an entire older generation on my husband's side. We have passed through not only the experiences of "the sandwich generation" but have become, with the exception of my ninety-year-old mother, the "older generation." We have endured the traumas of job loss, critical illness, and all the attendant complexities of negotiating over a quarter-century of marriage. Thus my perspective on the experience of family life is much richer and more complex than it was when I sat down thirteen years ago to explore the "spiritual experience of family."

In the book world, there is still a very real need for a perspective that links the language of family and the spiritual life that is not simply crisis management, self-help, pop psychology, or a conservative social agenda packaged in biblical allusions. There is, I believe, a need for works on family spirituality that are rooted in an appreciation of the deep and wise spiritual traditions to which we are heir. I see a need for works that do not confuse the spiritual life with techniques for tension reduction or with leisure time activity but instead probe human experience in family and challenge readers to wrestle with the great religious questions.

I trust that this book will be welcomed by those who are parents and who, like me, struggle to integrate family life and spiritual awareness. I hope as well that it will be of use to those who work with or minister to families, either in churches or in other pastoral settings. Finally, it is my hope that *Seasons of a Family's Life* will make a modest contribution to the ongoing discourse in the academic disciplines of practical theology and Christian spirituality, for the theoretical language of faith and lived experience are the two deep wells out of which, for generations, living water has been drawn.

For our daughters
Emily Frances
and
Elizabeth June

ACKNOWLEDGMENTS

Several stories in this narrative first saw the light of day in the journal *Family Ministry* in the following issues: Winter 1999, *13*(4); Summer 2000, *14*(2); Winter 2000, *14*(4); Summer 2001, *15*(2); and Winter 2001, *15*(4). Thanks are due to Diana Garland, editor of that journal and coordinator of this book series on Family Ministry for her encouragement of and enthusiasm about this book and my writing in general. The series is funded by the Lilly Endowment.

Essays originally published as "Memories of Now," "Passing Angels: The Gift of Spiritual Discernment," "Tears of a Greening Heart," "A Garden's Invitation," and "Potter and Clay" appeared in the following issues of *Weavings:* May-June 1995, *X*(3); Nov.-Dec. 1995, *X*(6); Mar.-Apr. 2000, *XV*(2); Jan.-Feb. 2001, *XVI*(1), and Mar.-Apr. 2002, *XVII*(2). The essays appear here in part or whole. The article originally titled "Living Contemplatively" was published in *The Merton Annual: Studies in Culture, Spirituality and Social Concerns,* 1997, *10,* pages 59–75. I have also incorporated "A Sacred Sense of Place: Reflections on Being at Home on the Plains" from *Practical Theology: Perspectives from the Plains,* edited by Michael G. Lawler and Gail S. Risch (Omaha: Creighton University Press, 2000), pages 16–32. Short essays previously titled "Easter, Love's Triumph Over Death" and "The Crib and the Cross" first appeared in *The Liguorian,* Apr. 2001, *89*(4) and Dec. 2001, *89*(10), respectively. "God-With-Us" was originally published in *The Lutheran,* Dec. 2000, *13*(2). All these, where necessary, are used with permission.

Barbara Braden, dean of Creighton's Graduate School, made possible the funds to allow Jackie Lynch of Omaha to lend her invaluable services to manuscript preparation. John O'Keefe, Theology Department chair, and Al Agresti, S.J., former dean of Creighton's College of Arts and Sciences, were gracious enough to permit some classroom release time for the completion of the manuscript. Sheryl Fullerton, Julianna Gustafson, and the editorial staff from Jossey-Bass have been thoughtful and gracious editors. I am in their debt.

Scripture passages are taken from the *New American Bible* unless otherwise indicated.

Chapter 1

SPIRITUAL FORMATION IN THE FAMILY
Living Contemplatively

> [T]he image of God is the summit of spiritual consciousness in [us] . . . it is [our] highest peak of self-realization. . . . To reach one's real self one must, in fact, be delivered by grace, virtue and asceticism from the illusory and false "self" whom we have created by our habits of selfishness and by our constant flights from reality. In order to find God, whom we can only find in and through the depths of our own soul, we must therefore find ourselves.
> — THOMAS MERTON

"It must be your vocation."

Her wise eyes peered intently at me as she drew her small self up within the wide folds of her monastic habit, readying herself for prayer.

We had been speaking in low tones in the anteroom of the monastery church on a Sunday afternoon. Outside, a gauze curtain of rain descended on the redwood forest. I had been filling the abbess in on the years since we had last talked at any length. Raising my three children—at that time they spanned the grade and high school years—had been the hardest thing I had ever done—also the most joyous, the most energizing, and the most enervating thing I had ever done. The abbess had not hesitated: "It must be your vocation," she declared.

Certainly, the first time I met this venerable woman the thought that childrearing might be my vocation was not one I could easily have entertained. It was 1976, and I had been drawn to this remote religious community hidden in the coastal redwood forests, enticed by quite another lure. In fact, as is the case with most spiritual journeys, I wasn't sure quite why I had come. I only knew beyond a shadow of a doubt that the silky seduction of solitude and the enveloping silence were like breathing pure oxygen. I had followed a tortuous path to arrive on the doorstep canopied by these ancient matriarchs of trees—a path through the big city, a thwarted theater career, one failed marriage, the interdisciplinary study of religion at the university, a long series of retreats, stays at monasteries, voluminous reading, earnest-if-haphazard spiritual practice of several kinds, and conversion to the Roman Catholic faith. The mentor who was to become my dissertation director had been to the monastery first and had jotted down these words on a postcard he had mailed from the remote Northern California post office: "September 8, feast of the Birth of Mary, a lone red rose sits on the altar. You would love it here."

So I went for a visit. And I returned for a stay of several months. And I did love it. Loved the austere yet comforting rhythms of the monastic day, punctuated by common sung prayer. Loved the containment of the tiny hermitage to which I returned each night. Loved the limitless expanse of heart and mind made accessible in the shared silence. But, as is the way of spiritual awakenings, personal issues gradually rose to consciousness in the void left where the usual frenetic distractions of life had once been. And I knew that I had come to learn that I had to go back to reclaim and reconsider the parts of my life I was avoiding by coming here. Yet I also knew that I was to go back differently, that whatever I had found in this redwood retreat was to return home with me to be lived, paradoxically, in a new, nonmonastic setting.

I had come with a keen sense of being called and, having arrived, knew myself to be called back home. That marriage and children waited at the end of my reverse journey I had no conscious clue. Strangely, that possibility had in fact surfaced while I was on my monastic retreat, but it was more as a metaphor than straightforward intimation. In the interstices between chores in the bakery or laundry and times of liturgical prayer, I found myself writing a fairy tale. Neither before nor since that time have I been a writer of fairy tales, but this one unfolded quite unbidden; a sirenlike, disembodied voice beckoned the narrator through fantasy landscapes and encounters with mythic animals. Finally, just before my leave taking, the narrative came to a close with the discovery, in a fictional meadow, of the voice's source—an elusive female figure who lay down on the ground and, thrusting one hand downward and the other upward, rooted herself in earth and sky, then was transformed into a sacred mountain.

It was not until I had returned home and the journey of my newly directed life began to unfold that I decoded the last image of that fairy tale. I had, even before the decoding, done a pen-and-ink drawing of the elusive "Witch of Gwendolyn," as I had named her—her long hair flowing out beside her mountain form like a rushing waterfall. Months later, as I turned the drawing on its side, I was jolted into recognition. I had created an image of a pregnant woman, her swelling belly rising above the earth on which she lay.

I cannot claim that motherhood has been my vocation in the sense that it is for many—the primary or sole identity-forming occupation in which I have been engaged throughout my life. I am also a wife, a daughter, a college professor, a writer, a singer, and a spiritual director. All these roles have shaped me. But motherhood has most profoundly formed me in the sense that "formation" has been classically understood in the world's spiritual traditions. Spiritual formation consists of conscious engagement in a series of spiritual practices that enable one to emerge as a transformed person. In the Christian tradition, spiritual formation has classically been about putting off the "old person" and becoming new in Christ. The tradition argues that human beings are created in the image and likeness of God yet have

3

been alienated from their original nature; the divine image is wounded, tarnished, or even effaced. The divine image within needs to be healed, cleansed, or restored, and the person of Jesus the Christ is at the center of this restoration.

Over the centuries, Christianity has splintered into various denominations over questions about how much we humans retain of that original divine image, how much we are able to and responsible for its restoration, and in what way Christ is present in that process. Be that as it may, in the tradition in which I locate myself (Roman Catholicism), it is affirmed that we have some part to play in our own spiritual growth. Although that growth is itself prompted by grace, our practices, thoughts, actions, and the company we keep do shape us.

There was a time in earlier centuries of the Christian community when it was assumed that true spiritual formation had to take place outside the ordinary routines of life; to be made new, one would have to "leave the world." Hence, from the third and fourth centuries on, spiritual seekers fled that "world" with its adverse formative powers—its greed, luxury, self-aggrandizement, lust for power—and entered into the silence and solitude of the Egyptian, Syrian, and Palestinian deserts or the cloisters of remote monastic hideaways. There they wrestled with those same adverse powers lodged in their own hearts. They sought to "die" to the false selves constructed by the "world" and to be reborn as persons animated by the Christ life, as persons of charity, humility, simplicity, and constant prayer.

Christianity has not been alone in having its set-apart masters of the spiritual life. Buddhism in its varied forms has its begging monks and its lamas or roshis. Islam has its Sufi orders. Hinduism has its saffron-robed renunciants and ascetic yogis. The Jain tradition has its sky-clad monks. All these traditions, through their most ardent practitioners, urge a profound spiritual transformation—a becoming what-one-is-at-present-not.

Of course, these traditions have more common paths to spiritual transformation as well. Each has its moral codes, its ritual worship, its religious expectations of "the householder." And, ideally, these common paths lead to transformation. But it is not always clear in what way they do. My sense is that the wisdom of spiritual transformation

4

cultivated in monasteries can shed some light on all of human life and encourage us to live more contemplatively. Not that one must "import" monastic life into the family (as if that were possible or even advisable) but that the general contemplative awareness cultivated in monastic life can bring depth to any human context, including family life.

———

In the winter of 1976, during that prolonged stay at the Trappist community in the redwood forests of Northern California, a clearer sense of what it might mean to live contemplatively began to emerge for me. That winter was a graced time in many respects. I lived a quasi-hermit's life, participating in the liturgical rhythm of the hours and in some form of manual labor during scheduled work hours. Beyond that, I was left free to rest in the impulse that had brought me there in the first place: the call to deeper solitude, the call to listen. I had been well advised by a psychologist friend before coming: "Don't think you even know the question you are asking by going. Just listen. Allow the various levels of conversation that constantly spin around in your head to gradually fall away to the point where silence itself is its own question. Never mind the answer." So I went. And I listened in that wonderful way that refuses to yield to analysis, commentary, or interpretation, where wind is wind and the beating of a heart is the beating of a heart and you realize you have never genuinely heard wind or a heartbeat before.

Winter is off-season for the community, so there were few guests. One week was even dedicated to a community retreat. A monk from a Trappist monastery on the East Coast arrived to conduct the days of reflection. In my listening mode, two things he said struck my ear with clarity and became the basis for my later understanding of the contemplative life. He evoked an image of a young woman seated in a meadow alone, breathing in the beauty around her. In fairness to the monk, I'm not sure what his intent was in bringing this particular, albeit classic, image to the attention of the community. But it provided me with an image for understanding what the contemplative life is *not*. A contemplative life may, in small part, be about the withdrawal to solitude and the aesthetic gaze upon the created universe. But it is not a life of idyllic fantasy, not something "other," not a safe haven from the harshness of the world. Nor can it be equated with a stress-free existence or a state of unalterable calm—with "being centered," as we say today. The other idea the monk presented has served me well in reflecting on a contemplative life. He said that such a life is about facts. It is about what is. But what we deem factual is shaped by our perception, and the contemplative eye sees "facts" with a certain stunning clarity. It "sees" into the various levels of reality down to the core where the deep silence pertains.

This contemplative approach is not necessarily synonymous with the term *contemplation* as it is used in traditional discussions of spiritual theology, especially those based on the writings of the sixteenth-century Carmelite mystics Teresa of Avila and John of the Cross. In these discussions, a distinction is made between "acquired" and "infused" contemplation. The infused type is equated with a lifestyle of withdrawal and an advanced state of interiority in which all human activity has ceased and the operation of God alone is evident. Instead, I am using the term in the way earlier authors like Augustine, Gregory the Great, and Bernard of Clairvaux used it, that is, as a way of perceiving the world—a simplified, whole seeing—that gives birth to faith, hope, and love—a way that tends to wordlessness and the unification of thought, feeling, and desire so that the energies of the whole person are gathered into focus. *Contemplation,* in this earlier Christian use of the term, might be defined as a listening awareness that allows the Word to take root in the heart and transform it. This is the way these ancient ones lived splendidly into the deep place that I sensed was central to my own life. Augustine gave it a name: "God is the life of the life of my soul."

It is easy to recognize the monastic roots of this concept as I have defined it. The ancient Benedictine practice of *lectio divina* (spiritual reading), to which the Trappist tradition was heir, involves the cultivation of a distinct sort of listening awareness. In the profound and sustained silence of monastic enclosure, where words are few and the words uttered are primal—they are God's Word—one cultivates a sense of the source of a given word's origin. One hones a sensitivity to

SEASONS OF A FAMILY'S LIFE

the primal utterance. In the measured discipline of monastic routine, with life's maintenance pared to a minimum, one can give oneself to the formative process of growing into the Word, letting the Word become the vessel into which one's life is poured. Or, to change the metaphor and stay even closer to the ancient tradition's self-understanding, the contemplative life is, first and foremost, a life of becoming a receptive vessel into which the divine Word is poured. Bernard of Clairvaux and his twelfth-century compatriots (to whom the Trappists looked as spiritual mentors), along with a host of other pray-ers in the tradition, likened themselves to the Virgin Mary at the moment of the annunciation, as recorded in the gospel of Luke: receptive, assenting, open to welcome the Spirit-seed that would inhabit, grow, and be born in her. The Virgin Mary is the model of the contemplative soul opening itself to God.

The contemplative life is a life of prayer. But it is a distinctive sort of prayer. Although related to other forms of prayer such as praise, petition, lament, intercession, or meditation, contemplative prayer has a quality distinctively its own. To put it plainly, in contemplation one allows oneself to be acted upon rather than to act as an agent. This allowing is not passivity; neither is it a cowering or a resignation to let whatever will be, be. Rather, it is a ready receptivity much like the readiness of the partner who follows in a couple's dance—who must be infinitely alert, instantaneously responsive, quick to dip and flow with the surge of the music and the practiced yet unpredictable step of the partner who leads. Such is the responsive readiness of contemplative prayer.

Such prayer risks much. To remain open to the influx of spirit is to be formed. To be formed is to enter into transformation. And contemplative prayer is about transformation, about being reshaped into the full persons we were created to be. To pray this way is to see, to hear, to perceive anew. The process of such a transformation is guided by the symbolic language of the cumulative spiritual tradition, but it is always unique, always irrepeatably particular. It is played out anew in each individual life. What can be said in all cases is that such a transformation allows one to enter into a particular relationship with what *is*. Reality is thus not approached primarily as a problem to be solved,

7

a cipher to be decoded, or data meant to be analyzed and controlled. Rather, reality is approached as a mystery to be plumbed, an astonishment etching its meaning on our hearts. This does not imply that contemplative prayer never issues in action or prompts us to wrestle vigorously with the problems of our world. On the contrary, the action that flows from contemplation can be focused and impassioned, intent on transforming the world. But the seeing of what is, the listening, the running of the heart's tentative fingers over the terrain of the real, is done with reverence and as an encounter with mystery.

Perhaps one of the most distinctive aspects of contemplative prayer is that, while we ourselves are being refashioned, God, as we have previously known God, also undergoes transformation. Or, to put it more accurately, we are led in contemplation beyond our earlier images and experiences of the divine. We are invited to continually let go of our familiar ways of knowing and encountering God. As we die to what we have been, God too seems to die. Thus the contemplative experience of dying, of penetrating deeper into reality and leaving behind all we have previously known, even at the seemingly most stable and foundational of levels, is simultaneously an entry into new, unfamiliar, less immediately apprehensible encounters with God.

To approach it from another vantage point: contemplative prayer has to do with allowing oneself to be formed by and made into an image that challenges the present images with which one lives. Contemplation invites vision that is constantly expanding; it offers a lens through which to gaze on life that inverts and subverts present perception and gives at least partial access to a "God's eye" view. Contemplation is that risky and radical opening of self to be changed by and into God's own self. Thus it is a life of continual dying, of shedding the comfortable and familiar over and over again, of being shaped by a reality beyond our own. From another perspective, it is a life of emerging spaciousness, of being made wide and broad and empty enough to hold the vast and magnificent and excruciating paradoxes of created life in the crucible of love.

On another monastic excursion to a Trappist foundation in upstate Oregon during my graduate school years, I was given a fresh image of the contemplative life that I find myself coming back to again and again. I had gone partly as an academic exercise—to become familiar with monastic praxis. But my heart was also trained on the inward dynamics I was experiencing. An inner grayness and a keen sense of absence had long plagued me. Analysis of the situation from many vantage points yielded nothing. I found it difficult to characterize what had been my sense of God for perhaps five years. "Gone" was perhaps the best description. I felt confused and alone, perhaps deluded. No one seemed to know what I meant. Then, during this classroom field trip, the young monk appointed to dialogue with our class illuminated my experience for me. We had been going around the circle, introducing ourselves, speaking in general ways about our religious backgrounds. I don't remember what I said, but he shot back, "Yes, I know what you mean. I've been there for a long time, too." And I knew that *he knew* exactly what I meant—knew that our truest experiences mirrored one another's. I was immediately confirmed and given hope.

I recall little of the rest of his conference except one phrase, which I later learned was a paraphrase of the poet Rainer Maria Rilke. But that phrase spoke volumes about where he and I found ourselves and about the nature of the contemplative life. "To be a Christian," he said, "is not to know all the answers. To be a Christian is to live in the part of the self where the question is being born." To be a Christian is to live into the questions, to push the horizon of self back so insistently that one's reference point is the ever-present act of birthing, to live in the presence of what can never be finished, found, or known, to live in God's time, open utterly to what is.

Contemplation is not an escape from the burdens of human existence. Rather, it brings us deeply into the heart of the world. Facts are the stuff of contemplation. But we must approach those facts with reverence, not primarily as problem solvers armed with our arsenals of established preconceptions but as people willing to allow God, through our practices and the events of our lives, to pry us open so that our seeing and our loving begin to mirror the clarity and compassion of God's.

Spiritual Formation in the Family

Very little in the structure and pace of modern American family life lends itself, in an obvious way, to a classic life of contemplation such as I have begun to outline here. If silence, solitude, and an unchanging daily rhythm has been understood in our tradition as the essential matrix within which to form contemplative awareness, ordinary family life would seem an unlikely context in which to speak of such formation. And, as we are acutely aware, historic Christianity emphatically affirmed that the monastery and the family were two dramatically opposed institutions. One was for prayer. The other was for populating a Christian society. I will never forget, as a young, recently married graduate student, picking up St. Jerome and reading his hurled invectives against the lot of the housewife: she, flying from one end of the house to the other, fretful over her spouse, her children, and her domestic duties. Where, fumed Jerome, is there time in all of this for thought of God?

This is not the place to chronicle the Christian religion's gradual, positive affirmation of marriage and family life as first a sacrament and second a place of prayer and the cultivation of a genuine spiritual life. This has occurred. The thundering rhetoric about family values that issues from the pulpits of all denominations is evidence enough of this. Yet there still remains much hesitancy about the compatibility between a contemplative life and life in a family. To the extent that we equate "contemplative" with "monastic," the hesitancy is an appropriate one. Family life, even if some members carve out solitary time and space or adopt rules about silence or follow daily rhythms of shared prayer, is quite different from its monastic counterpart. The spirituality born of monastic experience is primarily vertical and one-on-one (God and the individual); it implies a going apart, a renunciation of a life of intimacy with spouse and children, a relinquishment of property and the burdens of caretaking; it implies a certain marginality, a view from the critical distance that silence and solitude and spacious time allows.

A spirituality forged from the experience of life in a family, in contrast, is intensely horizontal; it is about the in-betweenness of persons, of relationships, about bodies and lives intertwined, the intimate proximity of others; it is about the busyness of tending and providing, about the stewarding of property; it allows for very little of the distanced perspective that silence and solitude offer.

Yet while monasticism and family life proceed from distinct and different human contexts and thus tend to give articulation to distinct spiritualities, there is nonetheless a significant sense in which both may be considered mediums through which a contemplative approach can be cultivated.

Although specifically monastic practices such as extended solitude and silence might be intentionally integrated into family life, I suggest that being quasi-monastic is not what lends itself to contemplation; rather, it is becoming aware of the natural contemplative moments and rhythms that present themselves in the daily course of life. Before I speak to these, however, I would observe that many of the practices in our society work against this awareness: the prevalence of constant noise, the omnipresent television, radio, and music, as well as the jarring din of city traffic so many of us live with. We also suffer from the lack of opportunity for self-reflection in most of our workdays, the frenetic pace of modern life, filled as it is with meetings, schedules, carpools, interruptions from e-mail, voice-mail, cell phones, the Internet, and answering machines. Contemporary family life is crosshatched by all of these obstacles to the simple, steady awareness of what is.

Blessedly, family life is not just about doing—about mortgages, grocery shopping, college education accounts, dance lessons, PTAs, child care, discipline, soccer leagues, or toilet training. It is first and foremost about the intense and tender and often fierce interrelatedness of human beings. It is about the astonishment of being with each other. It is especially through parenting that I have come to appreciate the contemplative dimension of my life. And although I have perhaps had more opportunity to be articulate, both to myself and others, about the nature of such a contemplative path, I am not alone in my intuitions. I have rarely met a reflective parent who does not immediately resonate with my descriptions of the contemplative nature of parenthood, even if their experience or language is not identical to mine.

If the contemplative life is about the steady gaze on the facts of existence—a gaze that searches for the still "I am" that undergirds all—then the family is certainly an arena that offers an uncushioned encounter with facts. To hold one's newborn child for the first time, to wait at the bedside of a dying parent, to suffer the agony of a life-threatening childhood illness, to delight completely in and with a beloved spouse, to hold ancient, treasured memories in common with a brother or sister—these are the simple facts of family. They are also sure gateways into the astonishing, painful, joy-filled facts of human existence—an existence whose very fabric is woven through with the threads of divine presence.

Perhaps it is because love binds us so closely in family that this deep piercing is possible: love, that gravitational pull that draws us out of the illusion that we are isolated selves; love, that primal knowledge of our common identity; love, that binder and healer of our shared alienation. Our false selves, resistant though they are, can be stripped away in the crucible of genuine love.

Family life does not have to be churchy or quasi-monastic to reveal its contemplative dimension. Some cultivation of self-reflection and the claiming of naturally occurring silent moments would seem to be essential. But these moments do not have to be superimposed. Rather, they need to be recognized, protected, and entered into. Routines of folding laundry, putting a child to bed with a song or story, fishing together on vacation, walking the dog on a summer's evening, driving in the country, watching the sun set from a porch swing, sleeping out under the stars—all these and a myriad of others thread through our lives together. They are breathing spaces—opportunities for the simple factuality of what is to present itself in all its unspeakable fullness.

Nor does a family have to fit the description of the perfect, nuclear, so-called functional family to give access to the sustaining, hidden ground of love. The persistent, onward thrusting of life itself seems determined to find expression in every conceivable circumstance. Most families know the times and places through which they have glimpsed that foundational love. Most families can name sacred moments unique to them. I think of a single mother who had escaped from a severely abusive marriage and who, along with her teenaged children, had grappled with substance abuse. This family's sacred time was at the kitchen counter, where they would stand in pairs, side-by-side, one washing and one drying the dishes. There, she claimed, the family could begin to speak and cultivate the communion they had lost for so long. Not facing one another (it was too soon for that), they experienced themselves "in a bubble," a time out of time when they could begin, together, to heal.

Although studies suggest that two-parent families tend to be the most stable environments in which to nurture children, I suggest that the *structure* of a family is not what guarantees its strength. There are abusive two-parent households and many wonderfully successful single-parent households. It is the commitment the family makes to living faithfully that makes it strong. In other words, grace is not necessarily embedded in any particular structure of family but, for Christians, in the arts of a life of love. A contemporary study of the Christian family conducted by two scholars, Lawler and Risch, makes this clear.

> *Agape* is willing and active love, self-love, courageous love, forgiving love, persevering and steadfast love. That is the love the Bible commands for Christians and, therefore, for all Christian families. It is worlds apart from the love into which many Americans "fall" and for which they often marry: involuntary, feeling love; self-getting and self-fulfilling love; self-aggrandizement love; happily-ever-after love (and if not, then split); unforgiving love; vacillating and temporary love. Although the Bible may not, as we have argued, have much to tell us about family *structures,* it has a great deal to tell us about interpersonal *processes* that make it possible for two or four or ten people to live together in family, peace, and communion.

Certainly, more formal disciplines of prayer can encourage the listening attention of contemplation. These will differ from family to family. Some may be overtly contemplative. A husband and wife may be students of Centering Prayer or Zen meditation and spell each other in babysitting duties so that they might each find time for their practice. Another family might have a shared ritual of morning prayer, dipping down into the vast well of the church's ancient liturgies to bring up the Word as a spring of living water. But not all members of a family may find cultivation of a specifically contemplative mode of prayer life giving. Some may have their faith energized through the exercise of social justice, through contact with the poor at a soup kitchen, or through community service. Others may find the path of intellectual engagement fruitful through a study of the spiritual and theological classics of tradition. In any of these cases, the contemplative undercurrent of our existence must be attended to in some way. That deep knowing is a portion of all experience. Awareness of it must thread through our study, our actions, and our interactions.

If I were asked to give a formal name to this contemplative living in family and to link it to the greater heritage of Christian prayer, I would first turn to the pages of the little Carmelite classic from late seventeenth-century France titled *The Practice of the Presence of God* by Brother Lawrence of the Resurrection. Lawrence was a lay brother of the Paris Carmel. His work in the community varied over the years. Among the jobs he held were sandalmaker and cook. Despite his obscure origins and the even more obscure role he played in his monastic community and the religious affairs of his era, Brother Lawrence had a wide reputation and was consulted for his spiritual counsel by many. He promoted a simple path, which he termed "the practice of the presence of God"—a habitual attentiveness to God in the midst of daily activity.

Amidst the hustle and bustle, the burdens and delights, the wrenching sorrow and unspeakable joy, all of us, monastic and lay alike, can follow the simple practice of finding God in all things. The contexts differ and thus the dynamics and insights differ as well. But the loving attention, the refusal to engage with life primarily as a problem to be solved, a cipher to be decoded, or a formula to be analyzed, the embrace of the facts of our existence as a question into which we live, a mystery we allow to enter and shape us—this we share. This is the contemplative life.

Two images, drawn from my own experience, suggest a contemplative claiming of our family lives. The initial image emerged during my first pregnancy. This was a luminous time for me, despite much fatigue and persistent sickness. I felt as if I were at the center of the universe, aligned with the most powerful generative forces of life itself (which of course I was). Fantasizing ahead to the unknown, I imaged an idyllic future with my child-to-be. In retrospect, this was rather like the idyllic image of contemplation, presented by the Trappist priest, of the young woman in a meadow, rapt in reverie. I saw myself as the mother of a cherubic, tow-headed toddler, sitting on a park bench as her child plays on the grassy knoll nearby. The whole scene is bathed in peace. Sunlight. Joy. I, free to reflect, am collected within myself, settled in delicious stillness as the beauteous young life cavorts in a pristine grassy, flower-filled park.

Real motherhood soon taught me that it is never like that. One is never free as a mother of a toddler, or a grade school child or adolescent for that matter, to simply sit back and observe. A toddler's outing to a park has to be negotiated around naps and meals. And one is always on one's feet, trailing or restraining an unsteady walker, alert for dog droppings, for obstacles that may cause tripping, for enticing glittering objects that may end up in a child's mouth. And one is burdened with extra jackets, diapers, snacks, drinks, a treasured toy that cannot be left at home—and always aware that fatigue, hunger, frustration, tears, or the need to use the restroom might strike at any minute.

Yet to see the world through the eyes of a child is to begin a lesson in wonder. To radically entrust your heart to another growing, changing human being is to risk living into the question. To know yourself as inextricably joined to another is to cross the threshold of the vast, inexpressible network of mystery that conjoins us all.

It is that mystery that brings me to my second image. In the fall of 1996, my husband and I sent our first child to college. It was an ordinary action, performed by hundreds of thousands of American parents each year. Yet for each parent-child configuration, the event is unique. Our daughter chose a Catholic university on the West Coast, halfway across the nation from our home. So the preparations and the dislocation were major. I went with her to see her settled in her dorm room, to hook up the computer, to help shop for what seemed like a thousand articles she needed to equip her to live independently from us. The university provided an excellent orientation program for new students and parents with just the right mixture of launching activities for students and letting-go pep talks for parents.

It was a good weekend but one in which I found myself struggling with the welter of paradoxical emotions that threaten to swamp anyone at a time of such profound transition. As the weekend progressed, my daughter was less and less at my side. A residence hall meeting, a first-year ice-breaker, a dance—these claimed her, as they should. Late afternoon of the weekend's end, I took a solitary walk out to the campus edge. Her university is situated on a wide bluff that overlooks the central city in one direction and the ocean in the other. Dusk was gathering, and I found myself full-throated with an explosive mixture of pride, sorrow, joy, grief, anxiety, and relief. I watched for a long time as the sun grew crimson over the sea, then started back to the central campus. As I rounded a tree on a grassy knoll, I noted a statue I had neglected previously. At first glance, it seemed to be a statue of the Virgin Mary, which in fact it was—but the Virgin as I had never seen her before. Standing, her body thrust slightly forward, arms lifted high, she offered up to the expansive sky an infant child. The gesture was at once tender and anguished, charged with the inexpressible, protective love of motherhood that must relinquish to an unknown future that which is more precious to her than life itself. The statue was dedicated "to the mothers of the university's students."

The statue was, for me, an image of family life—a variant of the contemplative life. Here was Mary, the classic Christian embodiment of contemplation, not before the conception at the moment of annunciation but after the gestation, birth, and nurture, offering all— her love, her life itself—back into the arms of the unknown. A radical entrusting to what is. Risking the mystery. Living into the question.

Chapter 2

STAYING AWAKE AFTER LUNCH

The Arts of Discernment

> Then the Lord said, "Go outside and stand on the mountain before the Lord; the Lord will be passing by." A strong and heavy wind was rending the mountains and crushing rocks before the Lord—but the Lord was not in the wind. After the wind there was an earthquake—but the Lord was not in the earthquake. After the earthquake there was fire—but the Lord was not in the fire. After the fire there was a tiny whispering sound. When he heard this, Elijah hid his face in this cloak and went and stood at the entrance of the cave.
> —1 Kings 19:11–13

Monday I sent our youngest out the door for his first full week of high school. He had risen especially early, had showered and eaten, and was standing in the pale light of morning near the living-room lamp, nervously organizing the contents of his backpack: a calculator with radicals for honors algebra, colorful spiralbound notebooks, the preferred fine-point pens, a pocket-size Spanish dictionary. Impulsively, I swooped down on his bowed head, enfolded him in my arms, and laid a kiss on the back of his exposed neck. He gave a slight shrug and a squirm. "Mom!" he pleaded, half embarrassed, half annoyed by the intrusion. I resumed a distance more conscious of the personal space needs of an emergent adolescent ego. "You look so nice, I couldn't resist," I apologized. And he did. Dress codes at his college preparatory school stipulate shirts with collars. His—a rich burgundy polo, fresh from the store—had a neat collar with pointed edges that still retained their not-yet-washed jauntiness. He looked wonderful.

I maintained the proper nonintrusive, maternal, hovering-in-the-domestic-background attitude for the ten minutes or so before his ride arrived. When the honk came, I peered around the edge of the archway separating the dining and living rooms. He had flung his pack up on his back and stuffed his house key in the pocket of his khakis. He opened the door, then uncharacteristically twisted back around, searching the room to see if I was there. He seemed relieved that I was. "Bye," he gestured awkwardly. "Have a great day," I smiled. Then with a click of the door latch he was gone.

The moments are at once so terribly mundane and so transparently sacred—ordinary moments that, for an instant, connect us to the depth, width, height, and length of love. Family life is full of them. It is also full of thousands of moments when love shows itself and we fail to notice. And it is full of thousands of moments in which we come face-to-face with love's painful absence. If there ever was a school of love, it is the family—a school not simply in the sense of an environment where information is passed on but an environment that profoundly forms us. There we not only learn our lessons in the arts of loving but we may be shaped, molded, converted, de- and re-constructed by love itself. We may welcome family members into our lives with hearts flung so wide that they seem to break, or we may only gradually have our hearts pried open to admit them. Either way, our families teach us, as no other teacher could, something of the spiritual life—something about the tenderness, ecstasy, and grief of love.

I have come to the conclusion that the fundamental art of the spiritual life is the art of paying attention. By this, I do not mean simply being aware of what is going on around you; I mean a contemplative attentiveness that is alive to both the outer and inner

SEASONS OF A FAMILY'S LIFE

dimensions of life and especially alive to the deep ground of silence that undergirds all that is, an attentiveness that can discern, amid all the noise and confusion, the still, small voice of God.

An attitude of attentiveness is cultivated over time and involves learning to listen on many levels simultaneously. The spiritual masters teach that this listening takes place "with an open heart," with a readiness to be reached, touched, and taught. One listens to others, to the Word of God as it is written, proclaimed, and lived; one listens to respected teachers, to the authority of tradition, to one's conscience and deepest desires, and finally and most foundationally, to the dynamic movement of the creative, whispering Spirit. In this listening, one begins to discern the differing qualities of the voices and thus to discern their origins. This classic practice is known as "the discernment of spirits."

A Summer Afternoon, Santa Barbara, 1977

From the porch, my view is azure and green, mottled with red and gold. At the horizon, the thin blue of the sky fades imperceptibly into the richer blue of the sea. The gradual descent of the land between myself and the distant shore is marked by descending tiers of trees: palms, jacaranda, and olives, with their muted greens of every shade: a canopy over the patchwork of adobe tile roofs. Gold bursts of sunlight caught by glass, metal, and water glitter and disappear.

Suddenly, I become aware of it: a flick, a brush. So swift and subtle I catch my breath and bring the swing to a full stop, hoping to feel it again. Yes, there it is again, like the touch of an angel's wing or feather passing in the breeze. For months now I have known. All the tests came back positive. The predictable physiological symptoms followed suit: the cessation of bleeding, the fatigue, nausea, tenderness, weight loss, then gain. But somehow it still did not feel real—more like a lingering illness than an impending birth.

But here, on this wooden porch swing on a summer's azure afternoon, I experience it and I do know. The momentary quickening—an angel's touch—from an aliveness at the root of my being speaks the volumes all the other assurances cannot.

Christians for centuries have not only listened to scripture but they have gazed on scripture as well in the stained glass, statuary, paintings, mosaics, and carvings that have adorned their places of worship. Thus they have experienced the Word of God not only as a narrative but as a series of visual moments—snapshots, so to speak— with which they pray. They have gazed at and into the images about them, not only to be informed of the story of faith but to be formed, to be changed by and into the images they behold. Among the images especially favored in the tradition is the annunciation—the image described in Luke of the young girl Mary, usually shown seated alone in a quiet room or open space, receiving an unexpected message from her angelic visitor. She is frequently depicted as bemused, startled, or humbled, yet always open to receive him. Her visitor is generally a majestic presence, unfurling his wide wings—never intrusive, always respectful of her reticence. The salutation is simple: Hail! The import of the greeting staggering: You shall bear a child, God's child. For generations of believers, Mary has been not only the chosen mother of the child Jesus but the model of the human soul in its most profound relationship with God. In her humble yet welcoming reception of the angel, she exemplifies the spiritual attitude that each person must adopt in order that God might become incarnate, might be implanted in human hearts and minds, gestate, be born, and made manifest in the world. Her free and chosen assent—her yes—mirrors the yes each one of us must give to become a mother of God, to become someone who bears divine life to the world. Mary is a woman visited, a woman made aware of the aliveness at the root of her being, the quickening within known through the touch of a passing angel's wing.

For centuries, Christians have sought the brush of wings, the assurance that God's life quickens in us. We ask, Where do we look? What does it feel like? How do we listen? Will we know? And we have named this inner art of paying attention. We call it "the discernment of spirits." Through time, we have honed the practice of this art, for it is at the core of the spiritual life. Although there are various methods or schools of thought on discernment, Ignatian, Quaker, San Juanist, in general it might be said that discernment is about two things: attentiveness and discrimination.

SEASONS OF A FAMILY'S LIFE

We have claimed that the spiritual life consists in paying attention to the Spirit of God moving in and among us and distinguishing that Spirit from the vast array of other spirits vying for our attention. These other spirits have been characterized as having a variety of origins: they may be spirits of the "world" (the purposes of normative culture that do not align with the purposes of God), spirits of the "flesh" (variously conceived as the addictive demands of bodily need or the egocentric demands of the self-absorbed life), or the spirit of the "evil one" (active forces working against good or the disordered meanderings of the human heart and mind that destroy and enslave rather than enliven and free). However the spirits are conceived, the Spirit of God is one touch, one inner brushing among many, and much of the work of the spiritual life consists in discerning which touch is which.

If it is to the annunciation of the angel Gabriel to the virgin in Nazareth that the church has looked to enact the dynamic of the human soul welcoming the Spirit of God, it has looked to another scriptural image to enact the drama of discernment. That image is of Jesus and his temptation in the wilderness. The three synoptic gospels (Matthew, Mark, and Luke) all contain accounts of this event. In each case, it is recorded as occurring immediately after Jesus' baptism by John the Baptist. Above the waters of the river Jordan, the Spirit descends and a voice declares that Jesus is God's beloved son. God's favor rests on him. The Spirit then prompts the favored one to venture into the wilderness for forty days. There he encounters Satan and his wiles. The temptations to change stones into bread in his hunger, to throw himself off a parapet so that angels will rescue him, and to worship Satan in exchange for all the kingdoms he surveys, have represented, in the minds of generations of interpreters, the temptations of power, pride, and possession.

To the prayerful viewer, the scene of the wilderness temptation is not only a narrative segment from Jesus' life but is a paradigmatic image on which to gaze to learn something of the nature of the human soul. It is an image of discernment. Jesus recognizes the nature of the attractive—in fact, alluring—invitations to procure what one hungers for—to be admired, even worshipped, and to own all imaginable goods. They are suggestions from a spirit different from

Staying Awake After Lunch

the one that compelled him into the desert in the first place. That first Spirit prompts him to refuse and to embrace powerlessness, humility, and poverty. When he had embraced these, scripture relays, he was ministered to by angels.

The wilderness scene gives a vivid, if not too subtle, image of the discrimination involved in discernment. It says that there are desert places into which we are invited by God where we will be asked to pay attention, to look deep into our lives, and to sort out the various motivations for our thoughts and actions. Of the many inner and outer voices that prompt us, which will we heed?

In traditional iconography, the baptism in the Jordan and the temptation in the wilderness are distinct. Stained-glass windows and altarpieces do not visually connect the two events. Yet, as narrative, scripture makes it clear that the two are inseparable. Jesus is baptized, the Spirit descends, the voice declares, "This is my beloved Son." Then that Spirit leads him out into the desert. Some time ago, while in retreat, I heard a reflection on this series of actions. It was significant, the preacher claimed, not only that the Spirit sent Jesus forth but that the Spirit sent him forth having heard that he was "child" and, perhaps even more important, that he was "beloved." It was this deep-rooted knowledge of belovedness that made the desert discernment possible. It was his identity as cherished child that enabled the carpenter from Nazareth to define himself as other than one who wields power, commands prestige, or holds wealth.

This insight arrests my attention. It says discernment is not simply about resisting what is evil, self-absorbed, or destructive. Discernment is about foundational identity. It is about who we know ourselves ultimately to be. It is about paying attention to the ways in which the limited power we wield, the modest respect we command, or the taken-for-granted resources we hold provide us with our sense of identity. To what extent do we "experience" ourselves primarily as civic and church leaders or as respectable citizens or conscientious parents or homeowners or degree holders or job holders and, only later or not at all, as beloved daughters and sons of God?

We are beloved not because of what we do. We are beloved because we are.

Discernment requires that we pay attention. An attentive pregnant woman pays attention on many levels. She is aware of the need for proper food, rest, and exercise for her body, which now must operate at peak capacity. She is aware, especially if she is a first-time mother, of the advice, stories, encouragement, and admonitions of doctors, relatives, and friends. She is aware of the changing configuration of her form, the new ways of moving and being that are required of her. She notes new thoughts and feelings, the dreams coming to be, the emerging fears, the changing relationships with her partner, parents, or siblings. She realizes she is changing. Her sense of who she is is changing. She feels the dynamism of the strong other growing within her—its habits and cycles, its enlarging demands. Perhaps she is attentive to the mystery of life itself that impinges more and more on her ordinary consciousness: the God questions, the life-and-death questions, the deep-joy and deep-grieving questions.

Discernment asks us to attend to what goes on around us and within us. Ideally, this attentiveness goes on much of the time, a sort of low-level, constant, spiritual sifting of the data of our experience. But there are times when discernment becomes much more focused, when a crossroad is reached or a choice called for. At times like these, the cumulative wisdom of tradition tells us to pay attention on many levels—to consult scripture, to seek the advice of trusted advisers, to heed the *sensus fidelium* (the collective sense of the faithful), to read widely and deeply the best ancient and contemporary thinking, to pray, to attend to the prick of conscience and to the yearnings and dreamings of our hearts, to watch, to wait, to listen.

Discernment is about discriminating—sifting through and evaluating the evidence of our focused attention. It is not, however, identical to problem solving. It is not simply a question of lining up the pros and cons concerning a particular decision we must make and then judging which choice is feasible or determining which gains the most support or which will benefit us, or others, in the long run. Discernment is more like the turning of the sunflower to the sun, or the intuitive hunch of the scientist seeking new and creative solutions for unexplainable, contradictory observations, or the restless seeking of a heart longing to find its way home to an estranged lover, or the artistry of the musician, sculptor, or choreographer delineating in sound, stone, or the human body the emergent, self-propellant, rightful line that says yes.

Discernment is about feeling texture, assessing weight, watching the plumb line, listening for overtones, searching for shards, feeling the quickening, surrendering to love. It is being grasped in the Spirit's arms and led in the rhythms of an unknown dance.

Middle of the Night in Winter, Omaha, 1995

I lie awake in the darkened bedroom, my husband's somnambulant breathing accompanied on and off by the onrush of sound from the forced-air heating ducts. I press my ear to the air space between these two respirations, where I hear the click of the key in the downstairs lock that signals my teenage daughter's arrival home, just before her 1 A.M. curfew. I try to read her step—cautious or self-assured, fatigued or energized? I note the tone of her response to my verbal welcome— hearty, irritated, ringing with contentment? Or tense and preoccupied?

It has been a roller-coaster year—not atypical, others assure me, but painful nonetheless, pressing all the buttons and boundaries that have been in place for some time. Her bedroom door snaps smartly shut behind her—an audible symbol of the unique, emergent psychic space she is structuring for herself. I stare into the dark void above the bed, aware now of my own breath, a light cadence like a descant above my sleeping spouse's airway melody and the furnace's punctuating bass.

In the last year, there have been many decisions to make about how to respond to the vigorous stretching of adolescent wings. We have received advice about tough love and about unconditional acceptance, admonitions to stand firm and to make space. We've muddled through on the level of "how to" and "what's best" and problem solving. But the level on which it has been perhaps the most challenging has been the level of spiritual discernment. By this I do not mean, What would God want the perfect family to look like? or

What are the proper roles that daughter, father, mother, and son are supposed to play? No, the spiritual discernment has been more akin to the sort of groping, confused reorientation I experienced as a first-time mother when the call was to recast myself as a parent, to learn painfully, by trial and error, not only the new psychological identity but the new spiritual challenges to which that identity called me.

The plumb-line question that has emerged in this recent process is, Where does love lie? I have learned a lot about myself (which, the spiritual masters say, is the beginning of knowing God). Now, having thought all along that I was cultivating a certain simplicity of person, I discover myself in fact to be a person very preoccupied with unfavorable appearances. My heretofore-always-commendable daughter has been brashly unconcerned about what anyone else thinks. And I have had to struggle to avoid seeing this primarily as a projection of my own inadequate parenting skills; I've struggled to let go of embarrassment about what others might think and keep faith with her in her uniqueness. "Can't you make this awkward transition a little less public?" I find myself thinking to her. But the question rips away my own precarious spiritualized mask. If it looks good, it must be good. Win God's and others' love by looking good. Cover up the deep wounds. Keep them private. Maybe they'll just go away. And I am forced back to the question, Where does love lie? The depth to which the question falls—the level of the Spirit's dancing—says, "Looking good is not the point. The point is, you don't earn belovedness. You receive it. It descends like a dove, unbidden, and you open your ears and heart and life and receive."

I have learned too that my cowardice—my fear of not being loved in return—can masquerade as maternal solicitude, that my inability to love the real wounds, the real out-of-boundness in myself because they seem unlovable is, in fact, a kind of spiritual pride, a closing in on myself away from the radical freedom and joy to which we are invited. I have groped about, asking, Where does love lie, and for whom and when and how? The hundreds of half-answers to the questions emerge only in the groping, only in the process of feeling texture, assessing weight, listening for overtones, feeling the quickening, surrendering to love.

When Jesus faced the temptations in the wilderness, he had just heard himself named as beloved child. What did he have to face in his own heart that kept him from knowing, from really embracing that truth? What groping did he do in the desert to find the level at which the Spirit moves free? What attentiveness, what discrimination was called for? Scripture says that when he was done, angels came and ministered to him. They must have done more than touch him as they passed; they must have unfurled their wings and beat the air and sung out for sheer joy.

Chapter 3

GOD-WITH-US

The "Family Altar"

> The gift of Christ's Body makes everyone a priest:
> because everyone can offer the Body of Christ on the
> altar of his own life.
> —Caryll Houselander

His prayer, not mine, is the one to which I return today. He had written it out in his nearly illegible hand on a half sheet of school-lined paper and left it for me, folded as an oblong packet at the foot of the hospital bed. It was the first *real* communiqué I had received from my husband since the Memorial Day previous when the physician's biopsy report had come back labeled "suspicious," and I had begun the series of tests and subsequently had survived two grueling thyroidectomies. He had, of course, been there all along, coping, rolling with the successive diagnostic punches, taking over the care of our three children, fielding phone calls from family and friends. But he had been sleepwalking, vaguely aware that he longed to wake up from what seemed like a bad dream. Now he addressed me directly, albeit in writing, and alluded to the gravity of the situation. The handwritten phrase, bent along the lines of the paper fold, read: "May you live to see your children's children."

My own prayer, uttered several weeks previous, had been at once more modest and more bold. It was a Thursday morning, and I had just stopped into the registrar's office at our eldest daughter's school between the end-of-school-year Mass and the annual Prize Day ceremony to place a phone call. The endocrinologist's nurse answered. Rather than provide a happy ending to several long weeks of inconclusive diagnoses as to the cause of the growth in my neck, she gave me the unsettling news that the consulting physicians agreed I should undergo surgery to remove a lump of "suspicious cells." I made my way into the school auditorium where the students at the all-girls parochial high school were lining up—a giggling pastel conga line in their gauzy summer frocks. As I watched our daughter, who was seated across the room, rise to receive a ribbon for excellence in freshman English, I counted the years I would need to see our youngest child through high school. Ten. Then, even though I know that prayer is anything but a bargaining tool, I bargained with God for the next ten years. More accurately, I simply informed the great mystery of divine life that I would be here, one way or another, until I saw our son receive his high school diploma.

Every succeeding year at that annual Prize Day event, first with the eldest then with her younger sister, I sent up a prayer of thanksgiving that I was able to be present. And I sorrowed when the mother of one of our eldest child's classmates, stricken with pancreatic cancer, did not survive to see her daughter graduate. Now, with both daughters launched and only two years remaining of our son's high school career, I find myself hoping that my husband's paraphrase of that ancient Psalmody has taken hold somewhere in the heart of the universe.

> May the Lord bless you from Zion
>> all the days of your life
> That you may share Jerusalem's joy
>> and live to see your children's children [Psalm 128:5–6]

This simple prayer, as poignant and as powerful today as it was when it was inscribed twenty-five hundred years ago, utters the longing at the heart of family life. Some of us do not survive to see our children's children. Some of our children do not have children. Some of our children do not survive. Or if they do, their lives do not bear the good fruit we hope they will. Despite this, the prayer laid on the altar of our hearts unites us: "May we see our children's children."

———

I have frequently been asked by groups to come and give a workshop or talk on the topic of family spirituality. One of the key components of such a workshop, as I have worked it out over the years, has been the ritual setting of a "family altar." Usually, I set it on a simple table in the room in which the workshop is to take place. I begin by explaining that it is an intrinsic part of being human to identify significant places and times where the sacred dimension of reality is felt to be especially and powerfully present. All the world's religious traditions have such communally recognized places and times. Focusing on place, we can recall that Christians and Jews alike look to the Holy Land as the numinous site where the sacred story of faith was first played out. When Muslims pray, they face the holy city of Mecca. Hindus revere the Ganges River as a spiritual site. Many Native Americans feel special reverence for their sacred burial grounds. Then there are the multitudes of other places of special spiritual significance: shrines, memorial sites, retreat centers, monasteries, pilgrimage routes. More locally, faith communities may look to the church itself as a sacred place, especially if the tradition acknowledges the presence of God as manifest there. People have "met God" at these sites and the sensibility lingers. By coming to them, one might also meet God.

The point is that humans, as religious beings, tend to locate the sacred in concrete locales where a sense of "the more" has been experienced. The same is true in families. A given family might name the dinner table as the place where that "more" is palpably present, that is, where the family is felt as more than the sum of its parts. Another family might name a grandparent's farm, or a cabin in the woods where they vacation each summer, or the car they travel in for a Christmas visit, or a bedside where nightly reading and prayer take place. The places are as unique and numerous as the families that claim them. But it is in and through the actual fabric of our lived experience that we come to know and touch a reality greater than we are: God.

Then I set the altar. I begin with a bare table and a background of gentle music. I choose a piano piece titled the "Nebraska Suite" by composer Rick Kuethe, who is a native of the Plains State in which I presently make my home. This music speaks of the particular locale in which my family and I reside. It expresses the fact that where we find ourselves is where we experience God.

One by one, a number of items from my own family's past emerge and are wordlessly arranged on the table. An antique Japanese swaddling blanket, given to my parents years ago by missionary friends, becomes an altar cloth. This pale-silk cloth swaddled me as an infant on my initial trip from the hospital and, in turn, swaddled each of my own children as my husband and I brought them home for the first time. The tiny white embroidered gown that my husband, now over six feet tall, wore on his christening day and that years later became the baptismal garment for our three tiny initiates is next. It carries the memories of my now-deceased mother- and father-in-law and their Kansas neighbor who lovingly fashioned the gown. A miniature "Team Star" baseball cap recalls my own father, who died in 1994, and my teenaged son. It speaks humorously to me of the primal mystery of "male bonding," for it came from my father—no sports fan he—on the occasion of the birth of *the* grandson.

Then there is the small icon my husband bought for me on the 1981 research trip we made to France when I was working on my dissertation. "Look at this," he exclaimed in a monastery gift shop in Dijon. "I've never seen a holy picture with a man and a woman embracing on it! The holy person is usually all alone or, if two are depicted, they are on opposite sides of the picture." This ancient icon of the church, the "Kiss at the Golden Gate," according to legend commemorates the meeting of Joachim and Ann, the barren couple destined in old age to become the parents of the Virgin Mary. Even without knowing the traditional story, the image spoke to my husband deeply of the holiness of a man and woman's love.

A homemade souvenir crafted by our middle daughter during her preschool days comes next. A fabric circle displays a small handprint in red paint—tiny compared to her college-aged hand. On the reverse side, a photocopied poem reads: "Sometimes you get discouraged because I am so small and always leave my fingerprints on furniture and walls, but every day I'm growing—I'll be grown up someday—and all those tiny handprints will surely fade away. So here's a final handprint just so you can recall exactly how my fingers looked when I was very small." Its paint now cracking around the edge, this treasure reminds me of its creator who, in fact, has always had a knack for leaving her distinctive adventurous impress, sometimes on situations she had best not been in!

And last, I lay out a young-girl-sized nightgown, hand-sewn from a swath of cotton that sports a print of the musical character Annie and her dog Sandy, surrounded by musical notes and scrolling song titles: "Tomorrow," "Easy Street," "Leapin' Lizards." This is here for our eldest, a new college graduate, and her grandmother (my mother), now past her ninetieth birthday. My mother spent a good portion of her life expressing her care for others through her sewing; my growing-up wardrobe bulged with her homemade fashions. When, years before, she had taken our eldest to a summer theater performance of the musical "Annie," she had commemorated the event by whipping up the "Annie" nightgown. Several months later, following a severe onset of macular degeneration (the eye condition that destroys central vision), my mother was visiting us and noticed (with some difficulty) that her granddaughter was heading for bed in the Annie nightgown. Offhandedly, she remarked that the gown was the last thing she had ever sewed. And so it remains the last thing my mother ever sewed. These ordinary objects speak more loudly than words: "It is in the ordinary fabric of our daily life that we experience the 'more.'"

The dressing of this family altar allows people to enter into their own families' experience of sacred space and time. Many can name the place in their own family's experience where they discover the more—the experience of being greater than the sum of the individual parts. Most of these name the dining-room or kitchen table. People say that they share more than food there; they tell of the day's events and extended generations gather together. They sense that the table becomes a place of encounter with the deeper springs of mystery out of which we live. Tables are places of communion, of mutual need and nourishment acted out on several levels simultaneously. Our physical, emotional, and spiritual hungers are fed in a mealtime ritual as ancient as humankind. The table itself becomes the sacred spot where the ritual is accomplished. That people feel this keenly has become obvious to me in the way people speak of tables. One gentleman I met in rural Nebraska recounted that he owned the dining-room table that had belonged to his great-grandfather. Every time he passed that table, he felt the presence of all the family members who had gathered there over the years. They were rediscovered in the presence of the table itself.

Tables are not the only sacred spaces of family life. Gardens, cars, bathrooms, vacation homes, tractors—the list is endless and varied. What they have in common is the fact that they are places of deep communion, of encountering others in a manner that exposes our primal vulnerability and hungers and makes of us both feeders and fed. We enact the mystery of our deep interconnectedness. This ushers us ultimately into our shared hunger for God.

Sacred times in family life have a quality similar to sacred places. Entering them, we discover the depth of our connectedness to spirit. Holiday celebrations and anniversaries are chief among sacred family times. They function for family members much the way the rhythm of the liturgical year functions in monastic life. They sanctify time. They pierce the opaqueness of ordinary time with a latticework of windows through which we peer into the depths of our lives. Year after year, we pierce more deeply, the celebration gaining in richness with each successive encounter; each time, we are greeted with all our previous experience—layer on layer. A wedding anniversary gains texture and weight through the seasons of a marriage. Encoded in that celebrative time are all the varied experiences of the years: the first flush of romance, the busy nurturance of birthing and childrearing, the excitement of the first house, the new job, the disappointments and failures, the reconciliations, the shared labors. The cumulative story is contained in time, not only of a couple's life together but of their most profound dreams, the music of the spirit, their dance with God.

Usually, a rich sharing of stories and uncovering of the mystery present in family life ensues from this workshop exercise. But at an event in the winter of 2000, attended by a wide variety of persons of different Christian denominations, most of whom were being trained for pastoral ministry, an interesting consideration arose. A gentleman asked a two-pronged question: What makes this sort of spiritual reflection Christian, and what differentiates it from sentimentality? Clearly, the question provoked some thought, for a fortnight later I received a letter from another participant still wrestling with these issues. I too have continued to mull this query over.

Truly, the temptation to trivialize lurks in any discussion of family spirituality. One example might suffice. An acquaintance of mine—a counselor by profession—reported recently on a session he had attended as part of a family ministry training program sponsored by the Catholic archdiocese in which he lives. A well-meaning speaker had been waxing rhapsodic on the way in which people might become true disciples of Jesus in their roles as parents. My acquaintance was taken aback when the speaker claimed that whenever parents diapered and dressed their baby, they were performing one of the traditional Christian works of mercy—clothing the naked. My friend was right to be jarred—not because tending one's own child cannot be a spiritual practice but because the traditional Christian works of mercy (to feed the hungry, give drink to the thirsty, clothe the naked, shelter the homeless, visit the sick, ransom the captive, bury the dead) generally refer to acts of mercy performed on behalf of the poor and marginalized, not for the benefit of one's relatives. These are acts of love—almsgiving in fact—that go well beyond what would be normally assumed as family responsibility. This caveat is well taken. Genuine spirituality is not sentimentality.

Yet at the core of one Christian tradition is the astonishing affirmation that "God is with us." That is the meaning of the wondrous name Emmanuel, which the gospel of Matthew bestows on the infant Jesus. In precisely what way God can be said to be with us has been variously understood and debated throughout the Christian centuries. I affirm this deep insight most broadly (and reveal my Roman Catholic denominational sensibilities as well) when I ask participants to feel around the texture of their family lives to discover the more. It is a first step, a beginning cultivation of the awareness that creation itself, which we claim is sustained in its very being by a divine creator, is transparent, can give us glimpses of an invisible depth not exhausted by the visible. It is precisely through the visible, the created, the stuff of life itself that we are initiated into the hidden ground that sustains us even if our seeing is clouded, even if our human weakness thwarts us. In family, it is specifically in the felt experience of relational love that we are first aware of the vast mystery of love that most aptly, if partially, hints at the nature of God. Of course the appellation Emmanuel, found in the gospel of Matthew, contains a more specific insight than that the presence of the divine can be intuited in our most profound experiences of human love. There is also a salvific claim, pointing to Jesus, to God incarnate, that God comes to us first as a helpless infant swaddled in a rough cloth.

I have found it profoundly helpful, when ministering to families, to begin with lived experience, that is, with those intimations of love with which our deep bonds in family might provide us. From there, family members go on to weave those experiences and stories into the overarching stories of faith. Who are we? Loving parents of these particular children? Children who love these discrete parents? Or, most significantly, children of a God who, the scriptures proclaim, is Love Itself.

Is this loving gaze into the stuff of our families' lives mere sentimentality? My correspondent arrived at that conclusion. For him, this contemplative feeling over the fabric of the real boiled down to a nostalgic reminiscence, an unreal identification of sacred presence with some idealized "sweet time" when children were young or we were innocent of the cares of life. Although I acknowledge that sentimentality can be a real danger not only in this exercise but in the spiritual or devotional life itself, I cannot agree with my correspondent. For it both conforms to my experience and is part of my theological repertoire to affirm that the innate human experience of intense longing is at root our longing for God. The concrete memories of loving persons and places and the items that evoke those memories are most truly the tactile threads that lead us back to our true home— that lead us back to God. Our *deepest* intuitions, guided by the wisdom of the faith, do not turn us into ourselves but orient us toward one another and, finally, toward our end and beginning, our God. We do this, not through bypassing the particular but by plunging deeply into it, by allowing it to become an earthen vessel that holds a treasure. The miniature white embroidered baptismal garment that enfolded my husband and children is, for me, not merely a cherished heirloom but a vibrant touchstone. Each time I touch it, I become once again an initiate; I rekindle the many knowings to which that garment points. The love that it awakens in me is not simply sentiment but a small yet powerful intimation of Love Itself.

Chapter 4

BIG STORY, LITTLE STORY
The Family Narrative

Be ready to listen to every narrative, and do not let wise
proverbs escape you.
—SIRACH 6:35 (REVISED STANDARD VERSION)

The marquee outside Calvary Baptist Church announces "The Best
Vitamin for a Christian: B1." Across the busy thoroughfare, the Salvation Army Renaissance Center advertises contemporary worship at
6:30 P.M., a full-service child-care center, skills programs for teen parents, and low-cost housing for the elderly. A block to the south, just
past a family-owned diner, a land survey office, and a stained-glass
artisan's workshop, the newly renovated gold-leaf roof of St. Cecilia
Roman Catholic Cathedral gleams in the morning shafts of sun. Two
blocks farther, a Saturday morning walk in our neighborhood takes
me past the quaint country parsonage of St. Barnabas Episcopal,
where last month High Tea and Solemn Vespers were celebrated in
honor of the queen's birthday.

If I were to make this walk very ambitious, I might head east,
toward downtown, where the sign outside the neat brick Reorganized
Church of the Latter Day Saints notes Friday evening informational

films; I might continue past the more modest stucco that houses Lighthouse Pentecostal and the tumbled-down storefront of the Tabernacle Church of God in Christ, which sports a crude hand-painted sign that reads, "Marvin Jones, Mattie Whitlock, Pastors." If I intended a more modest walk, I could head west, cross the wide lanes of Saddlecreek Boulevard with its cacophony of Burger King, Target, Walgreen's Drugs, Indian Creek Nursery, Subway, Arby's, and A-1 Auto Supplies and climb one of the rises of Omaha's rolling hills to find myself on the spacious grounds of Temple Israel—the Reformed variant of one of Omaha's five Jewish congregations. Here, monthly, I *do* come to engage in discussion at the meetings of the Jewish Catholic Dialogue Group. It is to this same neighborhood—to First Methodist, a "Reconciling Rainbow Congregation"—that I come on Monday nights for weekly practice with the River City Mixed Chorus.

Other Omaha neighborhoods and their places of worship welcome me and my students periodically. Across town on the site of a former country-style restaurant, the Indian Association of Nebraska is financing the construction of a multi-million-dollar marble temple, fashioned in the turreted style of Northern India. Here Omaha's Hindu, Jain, and Sikh communities gather for fellowship and, at alternate times with or without the presence of devotional images, engage in their respective worship practices. Closer to home, a modest, cleanly kept bungalow, just to the east of historic Augustana Lutheran's parking lot, houses the Nebraska Zen Center. Here the America-born Soto school master conducts morning and evening *zazen* (seated meditation), with his various pupils settled on square black mats.

America is home to innumerable communities of faith. And each of these communities, among the many functions they perform, offers to its members a vast and comprehensive narrative within which to orient their lives. They tell a cosmic story that provides the overarching plot within which the smaller stories of personal and family lives unfold. This is not the place to consider the compatibility or relative merits of the often-competing interpretive stories that faith communities tell. Suffice it to say that human beings, to live with any semblance of their full humanity, must live meaningfully. It must matter that one is alive. And it must matter in more than a passing way. If the history of humankind's ancient and ongoing religious quest tells us anything, it is that humanity experiences itself as (variously) created by, destined for, or awakening to some sacred dimension of reality. And, history tells us, from that reality we take our truest identity.

As a Christian, I understand my true identity as a child of God, created (to use the words of the book of Genesis) in the divine "image and likeness." The scriptural record provides a metaphorical word picture through which I glimpse my true created humanity, my alienation from my true self, the nature of a divine love that longs for reconciliation, and the gift of a long-ago child who illuminates the pathway by which I might fully become the child of God I am meant to be. It is true that different branches of Christianity tell the story slightly differently. Yet the basic dramatic sweep of the story line continues to be recounted in all of them.

The overarching stories of faith provide the larger context within which, throughout our lives, we continue to construct our personal and family narratives. This storytelling of ours is supremely significant. As one contemporary psychological theorist puts it,

> If you want to know me, then you must know my story, for my story defines who I am. And if *I* want to know *myself,* to gain insight into the meaning of my own life, then I, too, must come to know my own story. I must come to see in all its particulars the narrative of the self—the personal myth— that I have tacitly, even unconsciously, composed over the course of my years. It is a story I continue to revise, and tell to myself (and sometimes to others) as I go on living.
>
> We are all tellers of tales. We each seek to provide our scattered and often confusing experiences with a sense of coherence by arranging the episodes of our lives into stories. This is not the stuff of delusion or self-deception. We are not telling ourselves lies. Rather, through our personal [stories], each of us discovers what is true and what is meaningful in

life. In order to live well, with unity and purpose, we compose a heroic narrative of the self that illustrates essential truths about ourselves. Enduring human truths still reside primarily in [story], as they have done for centuries.

Our "living well" is played out in the interplay between the cosmic narratives of our faith traditions and our personal and familial storytelling.

Although they are hardly children anymore, our offspring are still enamored of family tales. Several paradigmatic ones surface periodically—the mischievous story of Dad as a youngster who, upon receiving a toy printer's set on Christmas, proceeded to set up his kit on the living-room rug, despite his mother's explicit instructions to the contrary and, of course, spill the ink; the yearly retellings of the stories of each child's birth; the poignant remembrances of Granddaddy Walter's summer visit to our new Midwest home when, at the first annual 36th Avenue block party, he wowed the crowd with his spirited performance with a foot-long bubble-making wand; the cautionary tale of the day on a long-ago Maine vacation when a slippage on a mountain overlook and a playground mishap almost lost us our two daughters.

Our stories tell us who we are and to whom we belong. So it is important that we tell stories—the small as well as the big stories. One family I know makes it a habit at breakfast on the morning of each child's birthday to retell the events of the first day of that offspring's life. Another single mother of an adopted child each year recounts the harrowing narrative of her trip to China to pick up her little girl. The humor, the drama, or the pathos of each of those days is forever etched in the family memory, marking the importance of the arrival of that individual for the whole. Photo albums or framed school pictures offer a visual narration of the changing configurations of family life and document the sometimes mundane, sometimes extraordinary events that constitute the narrative line of our lives. Each of our children has kept albums of the study trips they were privileged to take in their middle school and high school years. The eighth grade Washington, D.C., trips seem to feature as many images of gaggling, giggling groups of fourteen-year-olds as they do national monuments, but they do chronicle the early friendships and, retrospectively, the changing perspectives of each offspring. Now when they sort through these photos, my children explain, "I felt so grown up then, but how young I look!" or "I'd forgotten about Lauren (or Tom or Caroline), how sad (or remarkable or unexpected) their lives have turned out!" We are our stories.

Family stories do more than cement us together in remembered intimacy. Our stories also point to the values we hold dear. I will never forget the day our eldest came home from kindergarten with a graphing assignment. The class had in previous days made graphs of the fruit that the students brought to school in their lunchboxes: one column for apples, one for oranges, one for bananas. Now they were to prepare a graph of the various branches of the armed services in which their relatives had served. My husband was a college student during the Vietnam War and drew a high draft number on the lottery, so was never called up. His father was too old to be drafted for the First World War—a story in itself. Neither of us have brothers. But my own father was of eligible age during the Second World War. Deeply convinced of the futility of armed conflict, he risked imprisonment by registering as a conscientious objector and served the duration of the war in alternative service with the U.S. Forest Service. Our daughter's kindergarten teacher had to add a column to the graph. Alongside Army, Navy, Marines, Air Force, Coast Guard, and National Guard, she listed Conscientious Objector. The choices we have made become part of the family story. That narrative shapes each successive generation. For me, this legacy of conscientious objection has profoundly shaped my own thinking. Over the years, nonviolence, both as an academic area of interest and as spiritual discipline, has occupied my attention. And our son, now a junior in high school, has wrestled with his grandfather's legacy in his own conscience as he approaches the age at which he must register with the selective service.

Our stories are not simply individual stories. They are stories embedded in other stories; my personal story is part of the stories of my immediate family, my extended family, my local, regional, and

national communities, as well as part of the stories of my denominational faith tradition, which in its turn puts my little story in a universal, even cosmic, context. We need, I believe, sustaining narratives
on all these levels so that we might become people of character whose
lives have coherence and meaning. Families, among the other things
they are, are communities that tell the big as well as the little stories.

———

I laid aside the recent issue of *Newsweek* and gazed sadly out the living-room window to the street. April showers had not produced
many May flowers in our neighborhood, but they had transformed
the view from the window into a bower of greens—newly mown
grass, upstart bushes, tendriled vines, and freshly leafed trees—a celebration of the endless hues of spring green.

The article I had just read was concerned with the rising inci-
dence of teenaged suicide in America. Suicide has now surpassed
homicide as the leading cause of death among persons between the
ages of twelve and twenty-two. The journalist-author approached the
topic in a partly descriptive way, citing statistics. But he also focused
on a particular incident involving two teenaged boys from a Connecticut suburb who had planned and then executed a kamikaze-type
car ride into a tree. He had chronicled the effects of this event on the
community and conducted interviews with despairing teens of the
town. To his credit, the journalist did not attempt to present an easy
analysis of this bleak reality (Who can know the soul of a generation?),
but he did offer some statistical observations about young people who
attempt or accomplish suicide. Many are from broken homes, and
many of their families are uprooted often. But these are not impoverished children. They are members of the American middle class who
typically move every three years, dwell for a while in suburban housing tracts among other mobile families, then move on. What caught
my attention was the journalist's comment that few of the young people interviewed had any sense of belonging—to a family, a community, a tradition. They had no meaningful stories that could provide
any perspective from which to interpret the crisis of maturation.

In and of itself, moving from one place to another is not necessarily a bad thing. Nor are all divorced households breeding grounds for youthful despair. But both change in place and change in family continuity can work against the creation and sustenance of a coherent, ongoing narrative of life. And our lives are experienced as meaningful to the extent that they are undergirded by a narrative worthy of our deepest dreams. There is a great deal of public discussion today about values, character, and virtue. Important topics, yes. But persons of character and virtuousness who hold ethical values are not created in a vacuum. Nor are persons of character synonymous with "good" people who simply follow the rules. Character is constructed narratively.

One of the most cheapening aspects of contemporary American culture, and one that I believe acts to the detriment of families, is the commercial narrative that dominates our public life. It is evident in a thousand forms: in the ads that convince us that we may buy beauty and power; in the reduction of higher education to a purchased ticket to a lucrative job; in the insidious subtext of our upward social mobility (more and bigger is better); in the transformation of the public city green or square into the privately owned shopping mall; in our fascination with furtive information acquisition to the detriment of our spiritual, aesthetic, and intellectual formation; in our zeal to overload and overschedule our children so they will succeed in the competitive marketplace of life; in the extent to which we marginalize and underserve our "unproductive" citizens—the elderly, the young, the disabled, the poor; in the prevalent view that children and adequate health care properly belong only to those who have earned enough to have them; in our expensive purchases of new and better nipped, tucked, augmented, and reduced bodies; in our collective frenzy to cash in on a bullish market. We live with a powerful cultural narrative that defines us first and foremost as consumers and that locates ultimate meaning in the material things we are able to accumulate and display. The fact that Americans receive a stock market report on the daily news but not a report on indicators of child well-being is a striking witness to this fact.

Over against this commercial narrative, families and their faith communities provide an alternative narrative. We are not what

Big Story, Little Story

we buy, what we own, or what powerful positions we hold; we are an integral and interconnected part of a mysterious and graced reality. Communities of faith provide this variant vision through worship, scriptural accounts, disciplines, service, and devotions. We also learn the deep grammar of our faith traditions through the example of family members who have internalized that grammar. Marjorie Thompson, in her book *Family: The Forming Center*, puts it well:

> Many of us have been deeply affected by the evidences of faith we have seen in our parents or other significant family adults. There is something immediate and real about the life stories that emerge from our own family history. The ways a parent responds in faith to the loss of a spouse or a child, to a divorce, to a serious or chronic illness, to a truly wonderful or unexpected grace, to the tragic or miraculous events of life in the larger world—these create indelible impressions on children whose spirits are being formed in the web of family interaction as surely as are their psyches.
>
> Basic postures towards life, such as trust or fear, are indirectly communicated to children by adults, quite apart from the beliefs, doctrines, and morals they may be taught. Whether a child gradually becomes open and trusting or anxious and defensive in disposition has serious implications for the Christian spiritual life. In this respect we see that spiritual formation involves far more than what has typically been meant by catechesis or Christian education. It should be increasingly clear how central the role of significant adults within the home is to this kind of formation.

In Thompson's own case, her Presbyterian missionary parents with whom she grew up in Thailand provided a context in which faith as devotion, service, outreach, even sacrifice, was experienced every day. Less radically, or at least less geographically extreme, is my own father's witness to a nonviolent life. We live the stories we and our families tell.

August 2000, Omaha

It never ceases to amaze—all the things that parenting entails! The instance this morning was a fleeting one, trivial even. Last week my son, a high school sophomore, received the unexpected honor of a special recognition award that would pay full tuition for his junior year at the Jesuit College Preparatory School where he is enrolled. Needless to say, his father and I were thrilled for him. Listed on the letter of recognition he received were the names of the donors whose generosity had made the endowment that supplied the scholarship possible. Of course, he would write and thank them.

When we arrived home from the ceremony, I rummaged through our stash of stationery, found a box of embossed thank-you notes, and handed them over to our son. Several days later, on his way out the door to school, he waved in the direction of the piano bench (which also serves in our house as the mail and family notices depository). "I wrote my thank-yous. Would you put a stamp on them and mail them?" he asked. "Sure, I'll put a stamp on each," I replied. "Oh, you might need more than one on some of them." I paused. "What did you put inside?" "One has to go to Boston and another to Connecticut." I realized suddenly that he thought out-of-state mail cost more than in-state. "It's only more if it's heavier than a regular letter, unless it's overseas," I explained. He looked blank, then nodded. "OK," he said and slipped out the door.

Later, on my way out, I picked up the trio of letters. He had placed the small, elegantly embossed notes inside large legal-sized envelopes that he must have pulled out of our office supplies and addressed. With a start, it dawned on me that he probably didn't know that beneath the stack of embossed note cards in the stationery box were matching envelopes that fitted the cards handsomely. So I searched the office, found the box of notes, switched and addressed the smaller envelopes, slipped his messages inside, stamped each one (one stamp apiece), and left them under the red flag in the mailbox for the postal carrier to collect.

How, I wondered as I pulled out of the driveway, could *my* child be one month short of sixteen and not know the common customs of

Big Story, Little Story

sending a letter? True, he communicates with his peers primarily through electronic means, and a lot of his technological savvy is way beyond me. Still, despite all his superior college prep education, at which he excels, his parents should have clued him in to this basic life lesson. I stewed on this curious lacuna in my parenting all the way to work, reviewing scenes of myself and his older sisters laboriously addressing the inner and outer envelopes of high school and college announcements together or picking out decorative boxes of stationery in museum shops. Somehow, younger brother had missed out on these instructive sessions.

Late in the day, I found myself coming back to the letters. I cornered his sister in the bathroom while she was pinning up her hair for dance class and laughed about it with her. "Well, stationery *is* sort of a girl thing, I guess," she commented. But still I stewed. After a while, I knew it was not simply the specific incident that was causing anxiety but the by-now quarter-of-a-century-old anxiety that had gripped my life with the advent of our first child.

Its exact onset is etched in memory. Our infant daughter and I had been home from the hospital for several days. My main focus had been to learn the not-so-obvious art of breast-feeding. She was one of those infants who suckled briefly then fell asleep; then she'd wake again about an hour later to repeat the process. I was frantic, trying to ease her into a more rational pattern of feeding. Late one afternoon when my energy was at a low ebb, I picked her up and to my horror discovered a thin red line across her cheek, caused by her tiny wandering fingernails. And a small bubble of mucus was emerging from one of her little nostrils. Seasoned parents and caregivers will guffaw at my naiveté, but in that instant I grasped for the first time the truth that this little bundle in my arms was *my* responsibility. *I* would need to clip those offending nails (a thought that had never entered my mind during pregnancy), and, more terrifyingly, if this child was going to breathe, *I'd* have to be the one to operate the rubber syringe that had come home from the hospital in the plastic bag along with the talcum powder, ointment, and other manufacturers' samples.

As an only child of older parents who had hired a full-time nanny for their daughter's first two years, my experience in my family of origin had not prepared me for this realization. Nor, as a graduate student at the time, did I have a circle of women friends who were engaged in raising small children, although within six months I did make those necessary connections. My own wonderful mother had arrived at the scene of my daughter's birth full of energy but so far in years from her own "lying in" that her primary contribution consisted in bustling about our small apartment with rags and cleaner in hand, attacking every object in sight. My telephone had never before received such a thorough cleaning. In fact, I doubt if the idea of scrubbing a telephone had ever entered my mind.

My terror at all the unanticipated responsibilities of parenthood returned with a vengeance every time one of our children took a new developmental step. Who would have thought that they would be marked tardy at kindergarten if *I* didn't get them there on time; that they would suffer humiliation if *I* forgot it was our day to bring class treats; that they'd be kept from the class field trip if *I* had accidentally recycled the permission slip; that they might drown if *I* didn't make room on the summer calendar for swim lessons; that *I* would need to become knowledgeable about every obscure baseball, softball, and soccer field, track and cross-country course, and basketball and volleyball court within a hundred-mile radius of home; that their teeth would rot if *I* didn't set up and take them to those regular dental appointments; that they wouldn't know not to microwave tin foil or take a hair dryer into the bathtub if *I* didn't warn them; that *I'd* have to bone up on drug and alcohol abuse prevention; that just when I thought I was going to be able to sleep through the night again, teenagers' curfews would be keeping me up; that they wouldn't have a dorm room in college if *I* failed to correctly decode the mind-boggling hieroglyphics of the paperwork sent from a college of choice.

No one told me it was going to be like that. No one told me that I, who am only marginally competent at balancing my own checkbook and getting where I am supposed to be at any given hour of the day (assuming I haven't lost my calendar or my watch isn't off by an hour), would have to teach these little "blank slates" all the arts of competent living.

But that is the remarkable, unspeakable grace of it. To be entrusted with the care and nurture of another is to learn, through experience, not theory, the fundamental truth of our being, our true story. We are not best conceived as isolated individuals, out for "number one," but as part of an intertwined network of beings, responsible both for our own lives and for each other.

All the great spiritual traditions urge us into this realization, urge us to pierce beyond the confining limits of the ego-bound self to experience this deeper identity. "All my relations"—the refrain chanted repeatedly during the Native American purification ceremony in the close, dark, hot enclosure of the sweat lodge—echoes the insight gleaned in the transformative ritual. The Mahayana Buddhist tradition holds dear the "Bodhisattva vow" that its saints take—a compassionate vow to sacrifice Nirvana for the selfless life of leading others to enlightenment. "I must lead all beings to liberation, I will stay here to the end, even for the sake of one mortal being" the vow reads. In Christianity, the paradigmatic gesture that Jesus enacted during his Last Supper with his disciples—washing their feet—is mirrored over and over again in the tradition's history as men and women, in feeding the hungry, giving drink to the thirsty, clothing the naked, sheltering the homeless, visiting the sick, liberating the imprisoned, and caring for the dying take seriously his command, "As I have done for you, you should also do" (John 13:15 NAB). That gesture is translated into a more overtly spiritual idiom in the Christian monastic tradition, expressed this way by twentieth-century spiritual master Thomas Merton:

> Christianity . . . seek[s] to bring about a transformation of man's consciousness . . . and begin[s] with the consciousness of the individual. . . . The whole purpose of the monastic life is to teach men to live by love. The simple formula, which was so popular in the West, was the Augustinian formula of the translation of *cupiditas* into *caritas,* of self-centered love into an outgoing or other-centered love . . . fully open to all other persons.

Monastic life is expressly designed to facilitate this transformation of consciousness, as are other rituals and spiritual practices of the world's great religions. Disciplines of meditation, asceticism, prayer, and altruistic service are formative. They change those who engage in them. Likewise, if conceived as a spiritual discipline, parenting can urge us toward this other-centered awareness.

The spiritual transformation to which the great world traditions point is not merely domestic pleasantry; nor is it the achievement of an idyllic life cut off from the cares and concerns that occupy the great mass of humankind. It is a radical awakening to the truth of our human story, to our interdependence, to the fact that we are not discrete, isolated selves but mirrors of each other. This awakening is not confined by the walls of our domiciles. But it begins there.

Chapter 5

"MOM, STEVIE'S LOOKING OUT OF MY CAR WINDOW!"

The Spiritual Life in the Midst of It All

> It is an error . . . to wish to banish the devout life from the
> regiment of soldiers, the mechanic's shop, the court of
> princes, or the home of married persons. . . . True devotion
> . . . not only does no injury to one's vocation or occupation,
> but on the contrary adorns and beautifies it.
> —SAINT FRANCIS DE SALES

He is so earnest. In my office, his six-foot-two-inch, bearded young-
adult presence is large—not simply physically but psychically and
spiritually he looms large. The university course he is taking from me,
Living Religions of the World, has sparked his interest in practices of
Buddhist mindfulness, and he has stopped by during my office hours
to pursue his questions. Already at the age of twenty-two he has
achieved a firm, enthusiastic grasp of the Christian practice of contemplative prayer, and he is fascinated with comparisons between the

two traditions of spiritual practice. He wonders too if he should consider religious life. Recruitment posters from the Jesuit priests who founded this university are visible all around campus. And my student visitor articulates an interest in exploring monastic life. I do not know this young man well enough to discern whether he genuinely has a vocation to either the Catholic priesthood or monastic life or the celibacy they imply. I am aware that some are genuinely called in these ways. But when he ventures that he has always heard that if you really want to learn to pray you should embrace a celibate vocation, I laugh aloud: "You want to learn how to pray? Have children!"

Spirituality, in some people's minds and in some traditions, is often assumed to be about another, more ideal world or reality that is "above" the earthy tensions of ordinary life. In fact, for most people the spiritual life is carried out very much in the midst of such earthiness. I am not going to repeat the age-old and quite incorrect assertion that monasticism is all about selfish withdrawal. In fact, a healthy monastic life is very much an engaged life—a life of heightened awareness of the stark realities of human personal and social life. But it is not "ordinary" life in the usual sense in which we use that term. Ordinary life for most persons consists of a messy network of intertwined familial relationships. And that is precisely its challenge. Although I (with Saint Francis de Sales, quoted earlier, and many others) reject the ancient idea that the spiritual life can be fully carried out only in silence and celibate solitude, nevertheless the frantic busyness of contemporary society and the intense, embodied, relational quality of family life do offer their own distinct challenges and opportunities for grace.

For most of us, family life is a busy, bustling life filled with things to do and people to whom to attend. After the birth of our first daughter, I attended a new-mother's support group sponsored by the local hospital. Women whose infants had been born at the hospital between six and twelve weeks previous were invited to join. We met on Wednesday mornings at the home of a facilitator to share our experiences. What I remember most about the meetings (besides the carpet full of wiggling, squealing infants) was the common exasperation felt at being so busy. One wide-eyed young matron with twin daughters laughed as she described the highlight of a typical day: finding the time to get outside to the mailbox and bring in the mail. Even a daily shower was an accomplishment. Forget trying to blow-dry hair. Of course, what seems at first to be the all-consuming activity of infant care soon gives away to the ever-vigilant watchfulness of the toddler parent, the bedtime reading sessions of preschool days, the initiation into what will be decades of carpooling; school sports coaching; overseeing homework; keeping doctor, dentist, and orthodontist appointments; and attending parent-teacher conferences. Then there are the high school booster clubs, after-prom committees, math contests, dance recitals, piano lessons, summer soccer leagues, birthday parties, swimming lessons, the never-ending cooking, cleaning, and grocery shopping (for me an almost a daily necessity with a teenaged male). Top this off with headaches about insurance premiums, mortgage rates, tuition payments, money for new shoes—the list is endless—and it all adds up to a busy, busy life.

Yet in the midst of the busy-ness is a strange, wonderful stillness and a silence so full it dwarfs the chatter with which we fill our days. We sense that stillness as snapshot moments: we peer into the nursery of a sleeping infant, or attend the kindergarten class Christmas rendition of "The Friendly Beasts," or watch our high school senior parade across the stage and receive her diploma. In fact, it has been my experience that the very destabilizing of the self-preoccupied "me," the three-hundred-and-sixty-degree rotation in orientation that marriage and parenting bring with them, is in itself an initiation into a realm of being and loving that inches us, if we consciously allow it, into the deep ground of Being and Love that sustains us all. Again, it is in those brief snapshot moments—and I don't mean the cute photo-op moments—when the radical risk of genuinely loving another more than ourselves comes suddenly clear.

For me, the spiritual art of negotiating the busyness of family life has been twofold. First, I have in some sense surrendered to the fact that my life is essentially one of availability. When our children were young, I felt this most intensely in the twenty-four-hour-a-day, mom-on-call experience. This availability is still the key virtue of my family life, experienced chiefly now as an unexpected midnight phone

"Mom, Stevie's Looking Out of My Car Window!"

call from a distraught college-aged offspring or a family get-together orchestrated around the vision, hearing, and mobility limitations of elderly parents. However, I must make one vigorous disclaimer. Such availability must genuinely form us, not violate us. There will, no doubt, be for each of us critical times when we are stretched almost beyond our breaking points—times of serious family illness, financial distress, or unavoidable conflict. But availability does not mean being everything for everybody. It does not mean volunteering for every church, school, and civic project while you work full time. It does not mean letting family members take undue advantage of you. Husbands can pick up their own clothes; teenagers can fix their own lunches; even small children can be taught to respect another family member's need for privacy or time alone. The availability I'm talking about is not the doormat variety; it is a more profound willingness, in things essential, to be present to others in the family, to carry their deepest interests always in your mind, to attend thoughtfully to their genuine needs, and to have the contours of your own heart stretched by the unexpected, inexplicable particularity of each of those persons you have been given to love. In this lies the beginning of our being able to love as God has loved us.

The crucial discipline to be exercised, and the one I am constantly called to practice again and again, is found in distinguishing true availability from all the demands that claim us. Americans today live in what is perhaps the most speeded-up society ever to exist on earth. We are barraged by multitudinous, simultaneous instant messages about all the things we must have and must do. We overschedule our children so that they might be the best soccer, baseball, or football players, the most outstanding ballerinas, pianists, computer programmers, rocket scientists—or whatever. We overschedule ourselves so that we might have the best career, house, wardrobe, muscle tone, garden, or résumé. In our drive to have and do everything—immediately—we often seem to have forgotten that frenetic busyness is not synonymous with conscious and attentive care for each other.

The second spiritual art of a busy family life, next to genuine availability, is the art of cultivating our sense of the silence that undergirds it all. One might call this art Sabbath keeping. The idea of Sabbath keeping is, of course, embedded in the Jewish and Christian faiths. And where a family's religious observance encourages it to honor the Sabbath in traditional ways, it can be wonderful. The traditional Jewish Sabbath takes place from just before sundown Friday to just after sundown Saturday. Prohibitions from work and travel allow family relationships to become the center of focus for this most holy of days. Similarly, some Christian denominations have held Sunday (not simply the Sunday service) as a day set apart, during which faith and family are emphasized. But Sabbath keeping is not only the observance of a day. It is also about the cultivation of a certain quality of time. Sabbath time is gracious and still. It is spacious and restorative. It is not merely "time off" to refuel or run errands and is certainly not to be confused with noisy entertainment or frantic recreational activity.

Any time can be Sabbath time if it allows deep, rhythmic rest and rejuvenation to occur. Time set aside for gentle prayer or retreats, walks by the seashore, in a garden or through the woods, quiet afternoon moments sipping a cup of tea or reading a poem before a warming fire—all these and many more moments can be Sabbath time. They honor the stillness and silence that sustain our lives. When children are young, such moments may seem elusive, but afternoon naptime might provide a window of stillness. Or a spouse arriving home from work might offer to take over for a brief time so that the other can take a summer evening walk. What is perhaps most difficult for us is resisting the habit of automatically filling time with activity or filling space with noise. We race from commitment to commitment. Radios and televisions blare while we do housework and homework. We chat on our cell phones while we drive and walk. There are, of course, occasions on which such things are necessary. But I am convinced that the conscious cultivation of Sabbath time is essential to our being able to recognize those graced snapshot moments that continually occur in the midst of our busy family lives.

I am not suggesting that we must regularly schedule Sabbath time (although this might be ideal and might, for some, be possible) but that we must consciously and intentionally honor the need for such time. However we work that out in practice is for us to decide. One family I know has a practice of setting aside Monday evenings as

"Mom, Stevie's Looking Out of My Car Window!"

"goof-off" night in which all members participate. As our own children have grown, my husband and I have found ourselves on temperate Saturday or Sunday afternoons headed either north of town to Neale Woods—a nature preserve with miles of hiking trails—or out of town to some other wildlife preservation site where we soak in air and sun and the silence and stillness that drench the prairie landscape. Sabbath time allows us to enter the busy, cluttered parts of life with perspective and some equanimity.

Family life is not only busy but it is an intensely embodied life. Bodies jostling bodies for a place at the dinner table, bodies intermingling to create new bodies, which then inhabit one and then are held, carried, nursed, tended, bathed, and fed; bodies kissed for "boo-boos"; bodies patiently accommodated as they age and fail; bodies whose proximity one longs for and whose absence inflicts pain; bodies that keep one awake by crowding into bed on a stormy childhood winter night or keep one awake long past curfew in a sultry, adolescent summer; bodies that arrive unannounced for a fortnight's stay; bodies whose presence is required at holiday functions; bodies lithe and limber; bodies stiff and aching—the sacred realized in intense engagement with other bodies.

The classic spirituality of much of the Christian past in great part de-emphasized the body. Celibacy was the preferred state in life. And even where the body was a focus, it was in its disciplined control that the focus lay. Ascetic practices such as fasting and abstinence or more severe mortification and penitential practices were intended to subdue the passions (physical and psychological) and thus free the believer for the spiritual quest. The ordinary in-the-body life of a family member was the antithesis of that of the spiritual seeker. Certainly in the last several centuries, Christian spirituality has moved away from much of its negating, distrustful view of the human body. Parallel to this, a growing appreciation for marriage and family as a thoroughly Christian state in life has taken place. But, amazingly, there still lingers some doubt about the compatibility of family life and the spiritual quest. Even in denominations in which the celibate, ascetic life has not been held up as an ideal, the terms *family* and *spirituality* seem incompatible to many.

But it is precisely in the fleshy encounter that those of us who marry and have children are called to experience God. God is not met in our lives solely in the solitary one-on-one encounter or in some disembodied arena clearly demarcated from the fierce, conflicting pressures of daily life. To put it in the language of Christian theology, the mystery of incarnation itself—God becoming human—pushes us toward the insight that to encounter the infinite one most go through the finite—not around or above or below the finite—not by passing or eliminating the finite but through it, in all its unique, unrepeatable particularity. The finite and the infinite are thus simultaneously encountered. The startling claim of the incarnation, fully human, fully divine, becomes a lens through which all created reality can be apprehended. The finite, fleshy world is the privileged place of encounter with God.

Omaha, 1999

My mother-in-law came to live near us this past year, as it turned out for the last nine months of her life. Depending on how you conceptualize it, it was either the length of time necessary for a full gestation into her new life or it spanned the months of the school year's calendar—September to May. The last is perhaps the most apt conceptualization. She had, after all, been a schoolteacher for great spans of her ninety-four years: first as Miss Zirkle, Manhattan, Kansas', maiden seventh-grade English teacher, later as Mrs. Bergman, when she presided over freshman composition students at the university, finally as the favorite tutor of university foreign student wives to whom she taught English as a second language. The attendants at the skilled nursing facility reported that, almost to the end, she, in the most gracious manner imaginable, continued to correct their faulty grammar.

Not since our children were tiny has love been for me so utterly tactile, so much about the sheer mystery of embodied presence. A series of debilitating strokes had carried away the June Zirkle Bergman we had known. An MRI revealed that one entire half and a good portion of the other half of her brain was no longer receiving a supply of blood. Ordinary cognition could not have been possible. She had long

"Mom, Stevie's Looking Out of My Car Window!"

since lost the strength and ability to move anything but her left hand, which fluttered like a last desiccated autumn leaf, lifted by a light breeze. Speech and the capacity to swallow had ceased. Although her eyes remained open during daylight hours, she could not track my hand as I passed it before them.

All the qualities that had made her who she was, all that had identified her as grandma, mother, mother-in-law, teacher, and friend had vaporized in a surge of blood and bursting. What was left for us were the primal rituals of love learned long before at the bedsides of our children: the gentle touch, the low, rhythmic humming, the rocking, the waiting—waiting this time not for a future yet to unfold under our watchful gaze, at our table, on our stairs. This time we waited for another future. But the tender embodied arts of waiting were the same. As always, they connect us to the depth, width, height, and length of love.

Chapter 6

THE SCENT OF THE EUCALYPTUS TREES

A Sacred Sense of Place

Home is not a place, it is a posture, willing to be at home, whose forms in this life are never final and forever.
—Erazim Kohák

There are at least three distinct senses of home and one fourth, generic sense of home. . . . In the . . . "house sense," a home is a house, a domicile or residence, a dwelling place . . . in the "intentional community sense," a home is a self-consciously, deliberately chosen, familiar or accepted, abiding place of one's affections . . . in the "bioregional sense," home is a "bioregion" or natural place laced with local natural history and human lore . . . the fourth sense . . . is a house, intentional community, and bioregion where one's individual and community basic needs, life-affirming values, and sustaining relationships are met.
—Karen J. Warren

As United Flight 580 makes its final descent into Omaha's Eppley Airport, and I have buckled my seatbelt and put my tray table into its upright position, I strain over my seatmate's shoulder, trying to locate familiar landmarks: the nipped-off oxbow curve of the Missouri River that formed decades ago to become Carter Lake, the cathedral's twin spires that top the highest of the gentle hillocks rippling westward up from the Missouri's banks, the jutting prominence of the Woodman Tower that forms the axis for the modest cluster of high-rise office buildings that provide what Omaha has of city skyline.

This city on the plains, a century ago one of the great gateways of America's westward migration, has been home to me now for a dozen years. Each time I have reentered this place in the last decade, my sense of returning home has grown in depth and clarity. In fact, it has taken the better part of those years to begin to apply the rich, complex resonance of the term *home* at all to Omaha.

If, as poet-philosopher Gaston Bachelard suggests, home is "our corner of the world," a "nest," a "first cosmos," my sense of being a nestling, hovering over a womblike refuge, is quickened as the plane circles to make a descent that will return me to a longed-for spiritual, affective, and locational habitation. Cultural anthropologists argue that places capture experience and store it symbolically. Their claim powerfully corresponds to my own intuition. Place differs from mere space to the extent that experiences shape them meaningfully. For human beings, the ultimate place of experience is the body. We store our memories in muscles, mind, and cells. Beyond this, we store our memories in external places of intimate habitation. Thus home is the penultimate place of experience. Home is the place where we locate our sense of deep meaning, garnered from the past. Home is also the platform from which we interpret the present and envision the future.

But it is not merely my personal experience that gives meaning to a place, for places also store the memory of earlier inhabitants. That memory is encoded in the landscape itself, as well as through narrative traditions passed on in written and oral form. A true sense of a place involves the natural environment (which in its own right carries a unique history), the cultural environment (long and many-layered), my personal perception of the place (itself shaped by my sense of individual and collective identity), and the experiences I gather as I dwell in this place. Family relationships are central to this dwelling. Home, then, is the place crowded with the activity and aspirations of all the organic life that has and does concentrate in that specific locale and that I perceive as corresponding to my most primal identity.

My eye may seek the landmarks focused by Flight 580, but my heart hones in the direction of two other locations: the block-long neighborhood of 36th Avenue and the Platte River, which runs southeast just to the west of the city. It is in these two places that my sense of home is most focused.

———

The first of the places I call home is the block on which I live. In an older section of the city (as age is calculated here in this region, so late settled by immigrants of European descent), mine is a street defined by its shortness (one cannot drive or walk straight from either of its ends at Cass and Davenport Streets) and by its modest, older family dwellings sheltered by a profusion of towering trees. Our own house, located just south of the center of the block on its east side, is a circa 1920s two-story house (four-story if you include the finished basement and attic), whose original wood exterior is now covered with yellow vinyl siding and whose interior, catacombed by flights of staircases leading to the various floors, reveals the stages of the house's life. Within the house are demarcated the activities of its various inhabitants: original hardwood floors, now well worn and in need of refinishing; pine paneling added in the attic fifteen years ago by the young boarder fresh out of the military who kept himself busy fixing the place up; the newest coat of "wheat" semigloss latex wall paint (ours), layered over his flat white paint, layered (several coats) over the forest green paint preferred by the elderly widow who had deeded the house to her boarder, layered over a faded, flowered Victorian wallpaper applied by unknown residents to the walls of the house.

The changing configuration of my own family over the last decade is evidenced in the house as well. A basement storage area has been refurbished to provide a guest-bedroom space for the eldest daughter, now home from college only at holidays and summers, leaving her long-time attic bedroom free for her youngest sibling to move into (finally, at age thirteen) from the tiny nursery alcove that was his, up to the attic, freeing the alcove as an office for parents who have hitherto done their taxes at the kitchen counter and stored essential documents in the piano bench in the living room.

Sheltering the house on the southeast side is the generous embrace of a magnificent black walnut tree of uncertain age and ancestry. Its heavy presence hangs over the cluster of peonies, the row of fence-hugging hedges, and thin, graceful silhouettes of the redbud trees we have planted. Our house is both distinct from, yet clearly reminiscent of, all the other houses on our block. A few sturdy red-brick structures punctuate the neighborhood of wood-frame homes, representative of what local architectural historians call variously the "prairie box," "craftsman's bungalow," "California bungalow," or "foursquare" style.

The current residents on the block consist of several elderly widows or older couples who raised their many children here in this heavily Catholic city—persons who have seen the parade of infants become young people leave and empty the neighborhood of children, only to see again a new generation of families begin to move into the pleasant, modestly priced houses with roomy yards and plenty of bedrooms. Others who live here are those newer, younger families whose offspring streak joyously from lawn to lawn during the months of summer. There are a smattering of single people here as well—a fifty-ish rural transplant who wears a hunting cap and drives his ancient pickup down the street at the leisurely speed of five miles per hour, raising his forefinger off the steering wheel in neighborly greeting, as well as several midlife career women, seen chiefly going into then coming out of their doorways at a rapid pace, destined for corporate meetings.

Thirty-sixth Avenue is the sort of neighborhood where people walk their own dogs, plant their own tulips, and comment appreciatively on their neighbor's new roofing and disapprovingly on negligent summer lawn care. These are the descendants of the varied ethnic populations that first settled this city a century and a half ago—

Italians, Poles, Czechs, Bohemians, Irish, Germans, a smattering of Scandinavians, and later a small contingent of Hispanics and African Americans—drawn by the lure of homesteading, the advent of the Transcontinental Railroad, or the opportunities of the cattle industry.

This (to most observers) undistinguished block-long neighborhood is where my heart hones as I descend into Eppley Airport. But that homing in has a wider scope as well. For none of us truly inhabits a place by simply occupying space. Cultural geographers have posited that dwelling in a place inevitably involves a participation in its customary behavior or "habitude."

Habitude—the customary way of a place—provides a distinctive ethos. As a native of the metropolitan, multicultural sprawl of Los Angeles and a former resident of Boston, to me Omaha is a "big small town," not only because of its size (half a million) but because people here, especially in the old Cathedral neighborhood just west of downtown, behave the way small-town, mid-West inhabitants do. Many of the families on my block can boast connections with the area for several generations. I will never forget my amazement, the year we moved in, at discovering that our installation of a backyard swing set attracted a considerable audience of neighborhood residents, not all of them children, hanging over the back fence, exchanging pleasantries about the ramifications of our installation to their environment.

The economic range of households on our block spans the lower to mid-middle class. These are the insurance company employees, supermarket checkers, bank tellers, managers of venetian blind manufacturing plants, word processors, radiology technicians, and retired navy midshipmen of America. The 36th Avenue annual summer block party unfailingly features a keg of beer (paid for by shared donations), homemade deviled eggs, a green-bean and mushroom-soup casserole topped with chow mein noodles, as well as squirt gun drenchings by grade-school-aged children. Culturally conservative, these middle Americans maintain a certain historically grounded populist spirit. Most are churchgoing (predominantly Roman Catholic), outspokenly moralistic, unspeakably generous, and protective of those they consider their own.

The habits of being of these people who dwell on this formerly tall-grass prairie, despite the fact that most of them earn their living in urban blue- or white-collar jobs, are the habits of persons whose consciousness is formed by being workers of the earth. Conservatism, preservation, pragmatism, a certain skepticism about innovation, about ways that are too fast, too "citified," or too divorced from all that is settled, stable, and good—these are the values of an agricultural people whose survival is linked to the survival and fruitfulness of the land. Midwest religiosity is similarly of this strain. As our family has dwelt in this place, we too have absorbed something of this way of being.

———

From the air, I can glimpse beyond the city limits to the wide expanse of country that bioregionalists name the Dissected Till Plains—the far western fringe of what was natively the prairie just east of the Great Plains. In fact, unlike most of the aerial landscapes visible on both coasts of this continent, the region above which my plane hovers, with the exception of the city itself which spreads out for several miles, is basically rural and thinly populated. One can drive fifteen minutes north, twenty minutes south, and thirty minutes west from my downtown Omaha house and be in open country, most of which is under cultivation but much of which feels liminal and intersticial.

When I conjure up home, after the 36th Avenue neighborhood, it is this open countryside that recommends itself for my contemplation. For my personal and family sense of dwelling is complemented by the communal and ecological sense of sacred dwelling. Especially, I find myself focused on the River Platte, which slices a silver-green liquid swath through the land in a southeasterly direction just west and south of town. The Platte is in my mind both a carrier of deep cultural memory and the unique feature of landscape that defines for me the experience of genuinely dwelling in this particular place.

The headwaters of the Platte are discovered to the far west in the mountainous regions of Wyoming and Colorado where the North Platte and the South Platte, respectively, originate. These two waterways converge midstate to form the Platte. Its movement is eastward as it carries water off the eastern slopes of the Continental Divide across the gently descending plains to the Missouri, where the channel widens and the waters course southward toward their eventual destination in the Gulf of Mexico. But as a corridor of human movement, the Platte River basin has been, especially in the last century, a carrier of persons westward. The Great Platte River Road was the major corridor of American expansion during the era of the pioneers. It was a wide, flat, dry expanse of land that provided, in mountain-man James Clyman's 1824 estimation, "as firm a road as any in the Union or even in the world." Platte, in fact, is French for "flat" and is the translation French explorers made of "Nebraska," the Oto Indian name for the shallow-braided river that extends a thousand miles in length and is bordered on both sides by wide, dry, passable tracks of land.

Along this naturally available westward route surged vast numbers of people. Some were of Clyman's ilk—traders, trappers, teamsters—others were stagecoach drivers, Pony Express riders and stationkeepers; still others were soldiers, occupants of the many military outposts that dotted the treeless expanse of the plains. Some were explorers like Lewis and Clark or foreign observers like Englishman Richard Burton or American writers such as Francis Parkman and Mark Twain. Most were immigrants—persons whose principal objective was to cross the continent in ox- or horse-drawn canvas-covered wagons in search of a better life, whether it be in the form of the gold fields of California, the silver mines of Colorado, or the farms of Oregon. Some even came seeking salvation. Along the Platte corridor in 1848, the refugee church of Jesus Christ of the Latter Day Saints, under the charismatic leadership of Brigham Young, surged westward. They spent what Mormon sacred history calls "The Long Winter" encamped in what is now Omaha's northeast sector. Their martyrs, felled by the ferocity of the winter elements, lie buried in the historic Mormon Cemetery. The remains of other martyrs litter the Platte River trail as well, both Native American and immigrant, casualties of the sorry clash of cultures out of which modern America was born.

The Scent of the Eucalyptus Trees

Knowledge of the American westward movement, with its mythic images of wagon trains and hardy pioneers, was mine long before I ever set foot on Midwestern soil. It was part and parcel of an American education in my grade school era. If school Thanksgiving festivities were always recognizable by the paper pilgrims' hats and Indian headgear we constructed, so the end-of-school-year pageants always featured the fourth grade class dressing up pioneer fashion—girls in gingham dirndl skirts and pioneer bonnets, boys in farmers' overalls and plaid work shirts.

O don't you remember sweet Betsy from Pike?
Who crossed the tall mountains with her lover Ike.
With two yoke of oxen, a tall yeller dog,
A big Shanghai rooster and one spotted hog.
Singin' "Goodbye Pike County, Goodbye for a while."
We will come back and see you when we've panned out our pile.

Our singing gave voice to the nation's sense of manifest destiny. We patterned out the country's westward trekking to square dance rhythms. And on our imaginations were etched images from Laura Ingalls Wilder's *Little House* series, long before it was sentimentalized into a television program: young Laura, sunbonnet dangling in unladylike fashion down her back, hair flung wild with the force of prairie wind; her family's frantic search for baby Carrie, lost in the endless acres of impenetrable grasses; the grim, gaunt survival of the long, hard winter; the enticing torrents of Plum Creek that seduced and nearly carried Laura away.

For all the nationalistic romance of my youthful sense of this middle-prairie region of the continent, for all the fanfare that made the westward movement a part of an American civil religion, there was always an undercurrent of foreboding, hardship, and danger that surrounded the prairie myth. I will never forget the unrelieved starkness of Ole Rölvaag's novel, *Giants in the Earth,* that was part of my high school English curriculum. For there was not only the hardy, peripatetic traveler who passed through the prairie, there were the ones who settled to farm the land. Some, like the Ingalls, came claiming American identity. Others were immigrants. Forever etched on my spirit is the haggard figure of Rölvaag's pioneer widow poised at the doorway of her sod house as her sanity gradually leeched out into the bleak, featureless prairie spread before her.

This sense of the thinly veiled cruelty of this land was enforced by my choice of reading material upon arriving in Omaha in 1987. Willa Cather, claimed by Nebraska as one of its own authors, wove unforgettable word-tapestries of the immigrant prairie pioneers: Alexandra, the Bohemian mistress of the wild and often unyielding land, the bullet-riddled bodies of the ill-fated lovers Marie and Emil clasped in a last embrace, their inchoate yet expansive flight into what-might-be clipped by the narrowness of a provincial culture.

All these presences inhabit this place, their cultural memory made new through literature, oral tales, and museum displays. They are linked to me through our shared experience of this land. Although now it is altered by modern construction, this land still maintains its inexorable hold on its human inhabitants: the horizon-to-horizon expanse of the cloudless, eggshell-blue sky ("Nebraska blue" our family calls it); the fierce, icy grip of winter winds coursing from the northwest across the plains; the constant, subtle shifting of the River Platte from one season to the next, its slow, undramatic meander setting the pace for a Midwest culture as austere beneath as it is congenial on the surface.

Despite the fact that for most Americans, swathed as we are in the illusory veil of technological mastery of our environments, the natural landscape is perceived as mere backdrop or scenery to the air-conditioned, steel-girdered, jet-propelled enclosures that are our lives, the fact remains that environment shapes our subjectivity. Contemporary theologians have explored this process, noting the way in which the natural world—habitat—as well as the cultural milieu—habitude—play a central role in shaping our perception of the holy.

Environments are not interchangeable, and our sense of what sustains and animates created life, especially our sensibility of that sustenance, is shaped by the terrain we inhabit. Perhaps it is a truism to say that religious intuitions—our varied senses of the manifest form of sacred appearance—correspond to landscape. Yet how could the vast, silent stretches of the Arabian deserts give rise to anything but Islam—that iconoclastic celebration of the vast grandeur of the unknowable God? Why else was it that psycho-historical biographer Erik Erikson confessed that his great work on Mahatma Gandhi was, in fact, a transposed exploration of the spirit of Francis of Assisi because he had written it when on sabbatical in the Umbrian countryside? And why else, after many years' careful study of the life and writing of Saint Francis de Sales in California, when I received a grant to actually visit his Alpine homeland of Savoy, did I truly grasp his spiritual vision?

What might be the aspects of divine presence that are communicated through the typography of the plains? Perhaps these words hint at an answer: spaciousness, vastness, breadth, width, austerity, semi-aridity, harshness, emptiness. "Epiphany," a contemporary poem by Pem Kremer, captures this sense of the intimate relation between the shape of the land and the shape of God.

Lyn Schmidt says,
> she saw You once as prairie grass,
> Nebraska prairie grass;

> she climbed out of her car on a hot highway,
> leaned her butt on the nose of her car,
> looked out over one great flowing field,
> stretching beyond her sight until the horizon came:
> *vastness,* she says,
> responsive to the *slightest shift* of wind,
> > full of infinite change,
> > all One.

> She says when she can't pray
> She calls up Prairie Grass.

One lives surrounded by a sense of a fierce and lonesome beauty here on the plains. One lives as well with a sense of the unpredictability of the climate. With it always there is the wind, welcome in the wilting humidity of a summer's afternoon, fearsome in the icy grip of a winter storm. Yet beneath the fickle weather is the solidity and constancy of the earth itself—the material embodiment of what Thomas Merton termed "the hidden ground of love."

———

Nebraska is not the place I originally called home, nor did I immediately feel at home here. It was only after a decade of being in residence that any interior sense of deep homecoming accompanied my returnings, that I could look out an airplane window and sense that unmistakable faint release of tension in the region around my heart that signaled arrival at a place of origins. Since then, the complex, layered quality of experiencing a place to which one is not native as home has fascinated and perplexed me. It has occurred partly on the level of natural habitat, partly on the level of cultural environment, partly on the level of personal and familial life. The stage of life at which I find myself has something to do with it, as well as my sense of religious identity.

Southern California is the place where I was born. The metropolitan sprawl of central Los Angeles—districts between Hollywood and downtown, including Silver Lake, Griffith Park, and Echo Park—were home for twenty-six years. But the specific memories of those years do not radiate for me with a numinous sense of home, although they were good years and, especially in terms of my family of origin, fond ones. That numinous radiance emanates from a town further north on the California coast, Santa Barbara, where some of my most pivotal life commitments were made. I dwelt in the city hovered over by the mythic presence of Saint Barbara for ten years during my graduate school training. A conversion to the Roman Catholic Church, meeting and marriage to the man who was to be my life partner, the initiation of deep friendships with academic and spiritual mentors, the life-changing experience of first becoming a mother—these and other memories mark Santa Barbara as the place I most easily call home.

Yet when I moved from there—first to Boston, then to Omaha—it was not specific personal memories that provoked a sense of grief. It was the loss of the landscape itself. And that landscape included not merely the geographical features of Santa Barbara but those of the entire Southern California region. My mother used to call it "the Mediterranean climate." I feel it viscerally in the form of color, air, light, and topography. Nowhere else were those elusive olives and burnt-sierra hillsides, that dusky, adobe soil, the infinitely rich palette of somber gray-greens, dotted with magenta bougainvillea blossoms. Nowhere else were there electric-orange bursts of poppies on a chalk-gray field of dusty miller. Nowhere else was that unmistakable sense of being cradled between the coarse, tar-flecked sands of the Pacific shore and that arid, low-shrubbed range of hills. Nowhere else smelled of salt-sea air wafting over groves of pungent eucalyptus.

For a few years after I left Southern California, I missed friends and extended family. For a bit longer, I pined for the informal, leisurely lifestyle that the climate affords. A dozen years later, I still find myself startled into tears at an unexpected encounter with a jacaranda tree, an oak-lined walkway, a cut hydrangea blossom on display. To be on Southern California soil is to elicit a flood of personal memories but, even more inarticulately, it is to stand once again on the land from which I come. It is to stand on holy ground.

To possess a spiritual sense of place is in part to be sensitized to its deep history. A place may throb with sacred presence because something holy happened there—because it was the location of a sighting or the unfolding of a prophetic life. But places may also be sensed as sacred simply because they exist. As we bring to them a contemplative attitude, they may become numinous. To possess a spiritual sense of place is to be alive to "the isness of things."

It has taken the better part of the dozen years I have resided in Nebraska to begin to feel anything akin to a sense of home and, as with my sense of Southern California, it is the powerful lure of the natural landscape that convinces me that I am indeed at home here. The stretch of the Platte southwest of Omaha provided my first—and still is my primary—sense of the distinct bioregion in which I now dwell.

My favored points of entry into the long meander of the Platte are two short stretches of riverbank located a mile apart near Venice, Nebraska. Just beyond and before "The Merchant of Venice," a half-century-old wood farmhouse that now serves as a roadside stop for antique hunters, there are country roads leading to the left and right. The first of these guides you through the ranger station that marks the entry of Two Rivers State Park. After purchasing a day pass, you drive through the curlicue of gravel paths that loop around a small fishing lake, several groves set aside for picnickers, a cluster of retired Union Pacific cabooses converted into summer cabins, and recreational vehicle hook-up sites, until you find yourself at a dirt clearing that provides parking space for visitors wishing to spend a summer's day by the river. Wide sheltering torsos of cottonwoods dwarf the few bathers who loll on the scrubby grass, veneered with a thin layer of cotton wisps.

Before you is the Platte, perhaps a quarter-mile wide here, shallow as rivers go. How you reach it depends on the season. You find a temporary foothold along the muddy, ever-shifting sand that won't tangle you in an underwater trap of accumulating driftwood, jutting rocks, and sinkholes. If you find a foothold where the shifting riverbed sets high, you can wade out to the river's middle where the bed rises up above the water level, forming sandbars of varying lengths and shapes. In fact, when the water volume is low, usually in mid- to late summer, from the shore the river appears to be more sand than water—a crazy quilt of streamlets stretched over a blanket of gray, silted earth.

The second point of entry to the river is found by taking the right-hand country road, a brief quarter-mile around the bend to the retreat center operated by the Sisters of Mercy. Once on the property, you pass behind the pale-green, wooden, one-story structure that contains a half-dozen rooms for retreatants, venture out through the Saint Francis Peace Forest—an incipient grove of variegated trees trying to establish a foothold in the sandy soil, pass down a winding path cut through the low underbrush to another part of the riverbank, where the current might be slow and the water shallow enough to wade in. Here is found the great felled carcass of a cottonwood, which provides a rough-barked pier onto which the intrepid, crouched explorer can climb, hands clutching the remains of limbs, to arrive at a seated lookout from which the full expanse of the Platte's meander is visible.

The Scent of the Eucalyptus Trees

I am not a stranger to bodies of water. Growing up in Southern California, the Pacific was a constant presence, and more recent family hiking ventures have allowed familiarity with Rocky Mountain streams. But the Platte is utterly "other" as water goes. For one thing, its faces are legion. Only in summertime does it smile and beckon so graciously. Autumn's dipping temperatures make viewing the subtle fall color changes delightful from the bank, but the water by that time is dark and chill. Winter brings deathly cold. Chunks of ice float downstream in masses of pale-gray slush. Its January palette ranges from drab whites through ash and stone grays to steely blue. Spring returns a pastel blush to the water's surface, but runoff from distant mountains often causes the Platte to swell and rise, creating fast-moving currents that can carry an unsuspecting swimmer to a swift death.

Midsummer provides the window in time through which one can enter to become an intimate participant in the Platte's mysterious life. One can wade in the water then. This is like no other experience I know. From footholds on the bank, one steps into the deeper channels cut by the water's momentum along the edges of the channel. The sand beneath one's feet is dense and shifting; it forms a treacherous underwater terrain pockmarked with invisible rises and depressions, making each step toward the river's center a fearsome adventure. It is easy to lose one's balance and suddenly find oneself collapsed into an underground sinkhole or pulled every which way by small, swiftly forming whirlpools. But once one has eased away from the riverbank, calmer water at the river's central course allows one a rare experience. Summer days in Nebraska are muggy and hot, and the Platte's flowing waters are cool. Sandbars jut up steeply, and one emerges quickly from a full-body immersion onto a sandbar where water is lapping only around ankles and feet. As one walks, the immersion lessens and deepens, making one keenly aware of the moving, lapping line on calf, thigh, wrist, and shoulder blade, the changing threshold where moisture gives way to the tender brushes of warmed air.

A few hardcore sunbathers brave the entry ritual with lawn chairs hoisted safari-style on their heads, then lay themselves out on a convenient sandbar to toast under the low-lying sun. One can theoretically travel down the Platte on foot for miles, swimming lazily between the maze of sandbar islands that undulate up and down on the surface, trekking over stretches of damped-down, foam-flecked sand. Except for the occasional intrusion of a motorized pontoon boat, human sounds are absorbed by the musical slip-slapping at her shores, and the dense, almost desert silence of a sultry sun-drenched atmosphere hovers above the ribbon that is the river.

———

I have come once again to that small retreat house on the banks of the Platte, just north of Highway 92. I come with a sense of gratitude that a recent surgery makes it possible for me to anticipate a future with our children. It is late August and I realize that, of the many times I have visited this place, I have never managed to be here so late in the summer season; the roadsides are festooned with black-eyed yellow sunflowers—flora I do not associate with the place. It is a "quiet day," a break in scheduled programming that makes operation of the center possible, when closet solitaries like myself can come, wander, pray, sleep, and be bothered by no one. I rise early and venture out onto the property that borders the river. The place is littered with memories of the last decade. As I walk across the grassy field on my way to the riverward path, I pass a wooden placard that bears the names of donors instrumental in creating the "Peace Forest"—a project of my husband's while he was director of a small local nonprofit justice and peace organization. A perusal of the donor list brings to mind the deep history of peacemakers in this place. I conjure up the visage of Fr. Markoe, a Jesuit priest who, in the 1940s well before the civil rights movement had gained momentum, founded the Omaha student DePorres Club; the club's aim was to promote racial justice. A sideways glance at one of the planted trees that have survived brings to mind my elderly father, now five years gone, in the presence of his grandchildren, his hat shielding him from stifling heat and ferocious prairie wind, his foot bearing down on the lip of a shovel. He, the World War II conscientious objector, the lifelong peace activist, at the end of his life engaged in the never-ending generative performance of seeding the ground for new life, his sapling "peace tree" next to him cradled in the small arms of his preschool-aged granddaughter.

The narrow path cleared beneath the cottonwoods winds around a small pond. As I clear a familiar corner, I am startled by a new sight: the low-hung morning sunlight backlights a vast sea of gossamer-thin spider webs draped like party decorations about a wide field of tall grass, each web's unrepeatable, intricate pattern hung with thousands of tiny glistening lanterns—raindrops from a late night's thunderstorm waiting to be vaporized by the coming light of the sun.

The cottonwoods are heavy with leaves whose greenness longs to give way to yellow and brown. The damp warming air is alive with sound: the fat, lush rustling of late summer leaves teased by the wind, a cacophonous symphony of insect sounds—how I wish I knew enough to distinguish the cicadas, crickets, the various species of frog! As I round the edge of the lake, I recall a morning half a decade ago when the fall of my foot was the only sound for miles, when the cottonwoods were bare, gray-black silhouettes arching in embrace over the bright icy glare of the path made pillowy by a three-foot snowfall—my footprints, calf-deep, piercing deep hollows into the virgin snow. Grateful to be alive on this still, solitary walk, I gingerly fingered the fresh surgical wound pierced beneath the bandage wrapped around my throat.

At the next bend, I am reminded with a smile of an early spring morning, as a weary winter temporarily retreated and the sweet poignant wafts of new grass arose, when in a wild soul-weary impulse of desire for renewal, discovering a sun-flooded clearing shielded behind the brush, I stripped down to the barest hint of clothing and stretched out on the earth, letting shafts of spring light and a flood of tears burn and wash away the sins and sorrows of the previous year. This place on the Platte is the earthen vessel in which are carefully contained layer after layer of sacred sensing. This place, with the river that borders it, the city east of it with its block-long neighborhood, has become the place I call home. A decade of my personal and familial sacred story is encoded on this landscape. Each time I come here, it is both the same and always new. Each time there is a surprise: brown woolly caterpillars inching their way across the asphalt on the country road, the late evening apparition of a lone heron wading lakeside, a playground of chatty squirrels scampering up and down the cottonwood trunks, cheeks stuffed with seeds and acorns for winter storage. Each time I come, a new layer of knowing, a new piece of the unfolding story of my life is celebrated and prayed, stored for a time when remembering will be all there is. When the finite will render itself so transparent, infinity alone will remain.

Chapter 7

GENUFLECTION, PILGRIMAGE ROUTES, AND THE VACATION

Family Ritual

[I]t is difficult, perhaps impossible, and certainly unwise for human beings to attempt to engage in social and political life, or establish intimate relations, or educate the young, or have a religious life, or to make and enjoy artistic things without also making and performing rituals. Rituals belong to us, and we to them, as surely as do our language and culture. The human choice is not *whether* to ritualize, but when, how, where, and why.

—TOM T. DRIVER

"Will it be a 'real' Thanksgiving?" her voice half pleads over the phone. "Of course," I assure her. Our eldest is coming home for Thanksgiving holiday this year, something she has not always been able to do since she moved to the West Coast to attend college in 1996. "Real" means the way she remembers it, indeed, the way we have celebrated it for thirteen years since our move to Omaha from the

77

East Coast. Christmas is intimate, just for the immediate family—my husband and me, our three offspring, my mother, and, before they died, my father and my mother-in-law.

But Thanksgiving is big. Several other families and singles in the university community where we teach are, like us, transplants from other parts of the country, and we open the house for the Thanksgiving holiday. The number of revelers has varied over the years from twenty to thirty, depending on whether our regular guests have in-laws in for the season or not.

The living room, parlor, and dining areas of our house, all of which run together, are transformed for the occasion into a sea of decorated tables (our dining set expanded with three extra leaves, one card table in the central area, and a six-person folding table always provided by a neighbor wedged into the parlor). Lace tablecloths are unearthed from the cedar chest, and the two sets of hand-painted china bequeathed to me by grandparents on both maternal and paternal sides are laid out. My late mother-in-law's silver now graces the long table. Downstairs, in the finished basement, three card tables are set out with multicolored cloths and festive paper plates. It is there that the younger set dines.

Over the years the seating arrangements have varied. At first, the youngest children were placed in the living room near their parents' seats, and the older children were interspersed as supervisors among their midsize siblings in the basement. As the infants and toddlers grew into preschool and grade school children, they moved downstairs and the sprouting new high school students migrated upstairs to the adult tables. There have been years in which these arrangements have worked well and years in which chaos reigned. There was, for example, the Thanksgiving when two visiting grade school cousins came with one of the families and caused a weepy stir when they wanted to be seated together, thus dethroning a second grader who "always" had to sit next to her long-time school chum. Then there was the year a faction of the junior high crowd, unbeknownst to parents, dared one of the grade school boys to consume vast quantities of sparkling apple cider. He took the dare and the result was not pretty.

SEASONS OF A FAMILY'S LIFE

But whatever the particulars of a given year, the "real" Thanksgiving is big and noisy, chock-full of the aromas of roasting turkey, hot pumpkin pie, and Mother Standberg's Cranberry Relish (my husband's annual contribution). And it is deliciously crowded. It is a ritual occasion that we celebrate with joy.

Rituals of communal life are crucial to the well-being and identity of families. Too often the word *ritual* connotes an occasion that is routinized, boring, or artificial. But in fact, ritual behavior is deeply human behavior. Specialists in the field of ritual studies tell us that much of human culture is created of rituals; we agree to follow public and private patterns of behavior that make it possible for society to function. And rituals that are vital and meaningful contain many gifts. First, they are significant forces for establishing order in the world. This is not necessarily a rigid, stifling order but instead a harmonious, balanced order created in the midst of experience that is often chaotic and meaningless. Rituals are the pathways we tread to mark both the social and cosmic order of things.

Think of the central Christian religious ritual of the communion service or the celebration of the Eucharist. Although the theological underpinnings of these types of services differ, at the fundamental level of ritual both the Protestant communion service and the Catholic Eucharist are worship experiences that ground those present in the foundational story of Christian faith—the death and resurrection of Jesus—and enable them to enact the truth of that story. All are one in the body of Christ. God is present either in presence or remembrance. God's saving action in history and the final promised banquet of the end times is celebrated. The specificity of individual lives is contextualized, given cosmic significance in the performance of the paradigmatic gestures of feeding and being fed. In turn, the individual Christian must go forth and continue to enact this ritual, this nourishment, in the actions of daily life. Thus the overarching ritual order of reality orders worship and in turn spills out into every day.

Similarly, at the family table we ritually enact this primal human truth of our mutual need and nourishment. To come together around the supper table at the end of the day is to affirm that we are fed by

Genuflection, Pilgrimage Routes, and the Vacation

and feed one another. We share our daily bread. Our exchange is at once physical, intellectual, emotional, and spiritual. The gathering of the extended family for the yearly reunion weekend at the seashore or for a weekly Sunday afternoon supper at Grandmother's house sustains us as only rituals can.

Rituals also restore order when it has been lost. Recall how instinctively Americans headed for the nearest church or worship site at the time of the September 11, 2001, terrorist attacks. It was not only the emerging religious questions that prompted this flight but the deep human need for ritualization—in this case, for the ritual restoration of normalcy and the reordering of a coherent world through sacred words, patterns, and gestures. And recall how urban shrines replete with flowers and testimonies appeared spontaneously on street corners all over a traumatized New York City. Human beings must move through a ritual process to restore order to a disordered world. Think, for example, of the significance of funerals. We gather together to honor the life of a deceased loved one, and we ritually translate the body of the beloved into its new resting place. We lower the casket into the ground or carefully receive the cremated remains or travel to the place where the loved one was lost and, through prayer and gesture, bring ritual closure to the early phase of our grief. Anniversaries of a loved one's death are often ritualized through a visit to the cemetery or by publishing an "In Memoriam" notice in the local newspaper. In addition, rituals create community and unite us in an emotional bond that "consolidates relationships through intensifying the presence of one being to another." Weeping is appropriate at a funeral, as are the many other expressions of grief. The wake, so notable among Irish Catholic practices, or the tradition of "sitting shiva" in Judaism, creates an intentional environment in which a community of care is created around the bereaved, food is provided, memories are recalled, sorrow is voiced, and private mourning is honored and publicly shared.

Intimate family rituals that restore order—the family meeting, the "family hug," the late-night chat at bedside, or the comforting caucus across the miles over the phone—likewise can create community, uniting us in a bond simply by our presence to one another.

Summertime, Estes Park, Colorado

Before he pulls on two pairs of wool socks and laces up his hiking boots, he pumps the propane flame on the camp stove, heats coffee, and pours it into his insulated mug. His down vest snapped tight over the frayed plaid-flannel shirt, he heads up the hill behind our campsite for his dawn meditation. I remain below, curled in the canvas camp chair, clutching a mug of tea that steams my cheeks pink. Warm breath hangs for a moment then dissolves in the chill air. I pray here in the still time before our young people will clamor out of their tents and gather shivering at the wooden picnic table to wrap cold fingers around cups of hot chocolate, before he will appear from above, ambling down through the pine forest from his perch on the crags at the summit of the hill.

My prayer feels deeper here. In part, this is because we are in such intimate contact with the earth—bedded down on her firm flesh, scrambling daily over her treacherous stone outcroppings, cradled in her wildflower-strewn basins, cooled beside her dancing streams. But it is not merely this earth-intimacy that carves out a hollow in my prayer; it is the hollow etched out by our returning, our coming again and again to revisit this site, each time altered by age and experience. Layer after layer of our shared life is laid down in the storybook of this place. With the solemnity of ritual observance, we enact our parts. The steam from my tea rises visibly in the still air—rises like the incense of prayer.

The instinct to locate the sacred is a basic component of human religiosity. We store our "God-moments" in the locations in which they occur. Hence, religious traditions recognize holy ground—specific sites where one might expect to "meet God" or where the divine has been encountered in a special way. Further, human beings exhibit ritual behavior around sacred sites. The pilgrimage site is a prime example. Mecca is a powerful magnet drawing hundreds of thousands of Muslims yearly to its ancient confines. There the devout reenact the founding stories of Islam, wearing the pure white garments that erase cultural and class distinctions to make each one equal as "the teeth of a comb" in the eyes of Allah and exhibiting the personal restraint,

Genuflection, Pilgrimage Routes, and the Vacation

devotion, and transformed awareness that form the core of Muslim identity. Jews *daven* at the Wailing Wall in Jerusalem, remembering the destruction of Solomon's temple and pressing prayer cards between the chinks in the stones. At El Santuario de Chimayo, the most frequently visited pilgrimage site in North America, southwestern Catholics, some carrying heavy wooden crosses, make an arduous journey on foot during Holy Week toward the remote New Mexico shrine where, since 1816, miraculous healings are said to have taken place through contact with the "holy dirt" found in a pit behind the main altar.

In just the same way (although much less dramatically), families identify sacred places in their own lives. These sacred spots are often sites of important events central to the family narrative: an upstairs nursery where, in turn, each child in a family has spent his or her first years; the baptistery in the neighborhood church or the *bema* in the synagogue where family members were joyously initiated into the faith community; the fire ring at a campground where hymn singing brought everyone closer to God. Or there may be places that represent the gathered extended family—a grandparent's farm or a favored vacation cabin by the lake. Sacred sites may be places of memory—a garden first planted and lovingly tended by a now-deceased mother or a honeymoon cottage by the seashore. Or they may be places that evoke, in the course of daily life, the unspoken "more" that surrounds and sustains us as a community that is more than merely the sum of its parts.

I have been amazed over the years at the many different places —the sacred sites—where family members experience the "more" of their lives. The vacation site is a familiar one. I don't mean the one-time Disneyland vacation (although these can be great fun) but the site a family returns to year after year: a mountain campground, a lakeside trailer, a bungalow at the Cape. I have come to think about these sacred vacation sites as places of re-creation—places where the typical patterns of family interaction carried out in the routine of daily life (Who's got the carpool today? Did you remember your homework? How many times do I have to tell you? Can't you ever remember to turn off the lights when you leave a room?) give way to something else. Vacations take place far from our habituated sense of ourselves. Away, we often discover each other anew. Without the alarm clock that summons us to school and work, we ease into a day. We play. We enter into a mood of discovery. We eat meals we'd never eat at home. We wear clothes reserved for the occasion. We engage in activities foreign to our lives back in the city: playing miniature golf, fishing, hiking, snorkeling, body boarding, feeding the squirrels, taking lots of photos.

Our family inherited our vacation ritual from my husband's side of the clan. His father, a superintendent of schools in a small Kansas town, never faced the school year anew without first taking a trip to Estes Park in the Rocky Mountains. Back in the fifties and sixties, the westbound drive was a long one in an un-air-conditioned sedan. The destination was always the same: Budd and Gladys' Triple R housekeeping cabins where Dad would set up his horseshoe set and begin the games that would last all week long. My husband remembers rides on the Tiny Town train where the enthusiastic conductor, his knees tucked up under his chin as he crouched in his miniature engine, kept up a cheery patter to amuse his small passengers. He remembers picnics taken into the meadows shadowed by the great peaks of the Rockies and winding drives up Old Fall River Road to the top of the world above the tree line to the tundra, with its chill winds and carpet of alpine wildflowers. Photos inherited from my mother-in-law consist primarily of shots of family members at different stages in their development and in different configurations, framed against the majestic backdrop of Rocky Mountain National Park.

Years later, my husband and I honeymooned in those same Triple R cabins, although Bud and Gladys no longer were the proprietors. Then after a decade of life together in California and three years in Massachusetts, we moved to the Midwest; there my husband and I reinstated the ritual of the Estes Park vacation. At least biannually we pack up our children and head to the high timber, the thin mountain air, and the vistas that take your breath away. For a number of years, we were the houseguests of a friend whose own ancestors were founders of the Rocky Mountain National Park—forest rangers and early innkeepers whose dim photos were displayed in the

Genuflection, Pilgrimage Routes, and the Vacation

rough log cabin where we stayed. Later, when that opportunity disappeared, we began to camp in a campground nestled at the base of the National Park, well away from what was becoming a too-busy commercial center in downtown Estes. As our children have grown, we have accumulated camping equipment that gets unpacked in summer with the same wonder as the Christmas tree ornaments that we unfurl at home during the winter each year.

The trek to the Rockies has taken on numinous significance. As our children have become able, we have rented one "talking book" or another—Twain's *Huckleberry Finn,* Orwell's *Animal Farm,* Barbara Kingsolver's *Pigs in Heaven*—to listen to on the ride out. We generally stay overnight in Ogallala, a hamlet notable as a historic gateway to the Old West, complete with an authentic Boot Hill cemetery, a local diner that serves "Rocky Mountain Oysters," and an amateur summer melodrama for passing patrons.

A decade ago, we purchased a guidebook titled "Hiking the Rockies with Children," which is now liberally penciled-marked with notes labeling various hikes with the dates they were completed. We pull the book out each year and recall the stories behind the penciled dates: "That's the tundra walk we did when there were still snow fields covering the trail." "Remember when we met those backpackers coming up who had all their gear packed on lamas? And we had to scoot past those snorting creatures on that really narrow trail?" "That's the dismal one that's straight up! But it has a great view of the Big Horn Sheep breeding ground up top!"

Other pieces of the Rockies ritual involve must-do visits to the Tiny Town miniature golf course. We have gauged our competitive son's gradual capacity for frustration management over the years by his growing ability to lose at miniature golf in a sportsmanlike manner. (The trouble is that he got so good at it that he now almost always wins!) Equally as significant is the traditional trout pond experience and the subsequent fish feast at the home of our forest ranger friend. When we first went as a family to the Rockies, we had to contend with youngsters who lagged behind and couldn't keep up. Now I'm the one most likely to take longer on the trail and to meet up with impatient young people perched on a rock who query, "Where have you been?"

SEASONS OF A FAMILY'S LIFE

It is the ritual quality of this vacation, the returning again and again to a place that is at once familiar yet always new, that holds us in thrall. We love to discover unknown, adventure-filled places as well and have traveled individually or together to foreign parts. But the Estes Park vacation ritual is like no other. It is there that we enter time that's outside time. There we climb to thin-air heights halfway between earth and heaven. There we can see with the wide, long gaze of eagles the panoramic vistas that spread out below us. There the small, petty world that plays itself out below can be seen for what it is. It is there that the hollow being carved out in our hearts—that God-shaped hollow only God can fill—is ritually deepened, widened, and made more spacious.

Chapter 8

LIKE A RIVER
Rhythms of Continuity
and Change

[W]e must be so careful to meet our grace . . . if mine
depended on my going to a place to which I had the most
dreadful aversion, in that place there is a store of grace
waiting for me.
—SAINT ELIZABETH ANN SETON

Outside the dining-room window of the retreat house, a lone gray
squirrel appears. He scrambles up the trunk of a leafless cottonwood
to reach the small, cantilevered wood platform on which an ear of
dried corn is posted. There he feeds, casting nervous glances about
between mouthfuls.

Friday, the First Week of Lent, 2001

This Friday's landscape is painted with a palette of grays and whites.
A long, lingering winter landscape: the sky a shroud of pale-gray
haze; the silhouettes of bare trees displayed upon it like Balinese
shadow puppets; the retreat house grounds, where they are not
capped with snow, are a mat of gray-brown stubble. For a moment,

a flash of color enlivens the monochrome scene: a red cardinal pauses in his search for spring.

"And what of you?" he had asked the day before when we lunched at a local vegetarian restaurant. We had not lunched for much too long—he being busy with his duties as chief priest of the regional Soto school Zen center, I consumed by the frantic rounds of academic life. What of me? This was, I reflected, in one critical area at least, a waning time—a time of letting go. Our eldest daughter had the spring before graduated from college. We had just sent in a housing deposit that would secure a college dorm room for our second daughter. Our son, unlike his sisters, still was planted firmly at home, but as a high school sophomore was more and more away from the house. Near the home computer last week, I had found, penned in his hand, a list of intriguing college possibilities that, soon enough, would leave us empty-nested with the three of them flung far from coast to coast.

At dawn this morning, I bundled into layers of down and Polartec and ventured out into the pale light through the retreat house grounds to the edge of the river. How many times have I followed this same path across the open expanse of the Peace Forest, through the painted trellis that serves as an entrance to the wooded foot trails that circle around the small pond, then lead one down to the bank of the Platte? I have viewed the shallow river in many seasons but never in its present white, immobile state. Record precipitation and long months of freezing temperatures have left the Midwest ice- and snow-bound; the river shares in the region's crystallized fate.

This, I found myself telling my Buddhist lunch mate, is a new season. Children have occupied center vision for so many years now that it is odd to find them moving to peripheral vision in the course of day-to-day life. That is not to suggest that their positions have shifted in our hearts—far from it. There they remain at bull's-eye center. But for so many years their every waking moment was at focal attention: breakfast, lunch, dinner, bedtimes, and naptimes; diapers for bottoms and wool caps to cover ears, Valentine cards for the kindergarten class, evening gowns for the prom, carpools to soccer, basketball, volleyball, softball, and dance practices. There were homework

SEASONS OF A FAMILY'S LIFE

assignments and tooth-fairy surprises, Easter Bunny, Santa Claus, and birthday party decorations. Halloween costumes had to be sewn, new school uniforms hemmed, and babysitters found. There were "firsts": first tooth, first step, first spendover, first day of school, first communion, first sacrament of reconciliation, first driver's license, first date. And I spent much time monitoring piano practice, insisting on swimming lessons, signing report cards, cheering art awards and test scores, distributing play dough, breaking up back-seat fights on family vacations, drying tears, and shedding them; there were curfews and consequences, middle-of-the-nights with infant colic, middle-of-the-nights with oh-so adventurous teens. This is a new season.

For years now, I have thought about the twin dynamics of family spirituality as welcoming and letting go. For the past quarter of a century, welcoming has been the principle dynamic of my family life. In this season, letting go is the dominant note.

I am startled to have become part of the older generation. It happened virtually without my noticing. But as our eldest daughter's classmates begin to marry and baby showers replace college spring break trips on her social calendar, I am surprised to find myself in the been-there-done-that crowd. Yes, I am aware that plenty of firsts lie ahead—the titles "first-time mother of the bride" and "first-time grandmother" hold appeal. But these are situations in which I will play a secondary (though possibly crucial) role, and I will make the necessary psychic and spiritual readjustments, becoming a bit more the source of wisdom when it is requested, a bit less the determiner of events. When our children were infants, I used to look with some longing at the archetypal role of grandmother (spoil 'em and hand 'em back when they cry), for it was daunting to be the court of last resort, the one to whom the inconsolable bundle was handed when all else had failed. But it drew out all my gifts of comfort and nurture. It formed me. It drew from me those latent and hard-won capacities that transformed me from a woman into a mother. It taught me a way of being in the world that I have practiced for twenty-five years. And now something new is asked.

The pale wintry sunlight pierces through the haze, and a tiny flock of chickadees gathers beneath the cottonwood, plundering the corn spoils scattered by the now-vanished gray squirrel. As a Roman Catholic, I have developed a sensitivity to the continual changes of the church year. Lent—the forty-day period of preparation that precedes Easter—is a season for letting go. The purple banners and drapes that decorate the church sanctuary proclaim the penitential nature of the days. The traditional practices of giving up something like chocolate, alcohol, or meat is a straightforward way of observing what is the deeper meaning of the season. The giving up or letting go encouraged by this movement in the rhythm of the church year allows us to re-pattern ourselves. We are to re-align, re-assess, re-consider, re-form, and re-new ourselves. This requires that we relinquish old ways of being. These ways may be unhealthy and constricting or they may simply be ways that circumstance has rendered obsolete. This is a season for letting go.

I can't claim that at the other end of my intensive parenting years—the season of welcoming—the transition was any easier. I have a vivid memory of sitting in the pale-green kitchen of our first apartment at the breakfast table that overlooked our backyard in perhaps the second month of our first daughter's life. For weeks I had been barely functional, exhausted from lack of sleep and having become what can only be described as a basket case from tending a high-need, colicky baby. On top of that, breast-feeding, which in the seventies in Southern California was considered the only option for a responsible new mother, was going poorly. I was still experiencing some disorientation from the residual anesthetic that had been administered during an emergency Caesarean section. To top it off, it had rained since the day we came home from the hospital. Each day was endless. Making it to the bathroom unencumbered with a wailing infant was the most I could hope for myself in a given morning. Forget taking a shower. Forget preparing a real meal. Forget having a coherent thought constructed of more than three words. Forget ordering my environment beyond tossing the accumulated dirty dishes in a tub of soapy water or hauling the overflowing diaper pail to the front stoop for pick-up. Forget anything I had known as a pleasant, ordinary day.

I remember sitting at the breakfast table, clutching our firstborn, in my then-usual disheveled state, the walls weaving slightly in and out before me. A very cheery, slightly older, red-haired woman was standing in the doorway. I can't recall why she was there—an insurance policy or some such thing had brought her to our house. In my diminished state, I experienced her as an alien from another universe—a competent, energetic, organized person who swept into my slovenly world sporting an immaculate business suit and manicured nails. She was all smiles in her visit and tried to cross the chasm between us by reminiscing happily about the blissful infancy of her apparently perfect son. As she stood up to leave, she turned to me with a radiant glow: "Don't you just *love* every minute of this?" Then she swept out the door, leaving an odor of expensive cologne and bad greeting card sentimentality. I was left wondering what in heaven's name was wrong with me.

The welcoming part was hard. Perhaps if it had been second nature or if our first baby had slept through her early days, I never would have thought about motherhood as spiritual formation, although my experience has been that people *do* experience it in this radical way, whether they have given birth to a "good baby" or not. But my choice was either to give up on any semblance of a spiritual life or to find what America-born Roman Catholic saint Elizabeth Seton so aptly called the "grace of the moment." "Run to meet your grace," she used to counsel those entrusted to her spiritual care. Run to meet your grace, whether you are called to welcome or to let go.

The point is that the spiritual life is very much a life attuned to the present moment. And the experience of family is a vessel that forms us in that life, both through its continuities and its changes. There is something profoundly stable and rooted about faithfulness in family. We must be available to provide a dwelling place, a home, for those persons we are given to love intimately. Children need roots before they can sprout wings. They need to be able to trust that the world into which they have been thrust is trustworthy. Although that does not necessarily demand that all families replicate the "Leave It to Beaver" household, it does mean that serious attention must be paid to the creation of a stable community, shared rituals and traditions, and the experience of having a home. If the spiritual life has often been imaged as journey, pilgrimage, or exile, a spirituality of family must balance this imagery with an attentive consideration of dwelling.

At the same time it is concerned with continuity, family spirituality is also about change. The family unit itself constantly changes along with its needs, problems, and orientation. It is a challenge just to keep up with the varying demands of each stage of the family life cycle. Yet there are distinctive gifts—spiritual gifts I believe—that are offered to those who parent the next generation. These gifts are wrung from us in the crucible of love itself. Parental love is a powerful generative form of love that changes us as we explore its contours over the course of a lifetime. Among the gifts I would name is the capacity for flexibility. These gifts are not a matter of theory but a matter of the heart. Flexibility might also be termed *developmental sensitivity*. Over the course of a lifetime, parenting is not a single experience; different stages of the life cycle call for differing parenting skills. Toddlers need us in very different ways than our teenagers do. Parents, whether they are naturally better at parenting infants or adult children, are called upon to develop a love that can grow and change in response to their offspring's changing needs.

Parenting also requires us to love and nurture different personalities. No two children are alike. But to love a particular child means we must take her unique interests to heart, concern ourselves with his special problems. Parental love is manifold, changing, boldly adaptable in response to each individual child. There is an art to staying flexible and adventurous enough to continue to love in the myriad ways that being a parent requires.

This sort of flexibility requires that we be able to respond, or at least try to respond, to the new grace that is available in every changing moment of our lives. At times the grace may be obvious, delicious, wonderful. At times it may be obscure or pain-filled; it may elude our present grasp. It is especially those elusive moments, when God feels distant and when our experience outstrips our present capacity to practice the presence of the sacred, that we grow. That growth is not merely emotional and intellectual; it is distinctly spiritual if we allow it to be so.

That hard-won growth may be understood, from a Christian perspective, to have a cruciform shape and to encourage a greater intimacy with the divine. In her *Dark Night Journey: Inward Re-Patterning Toward a Life Centered in God,* the late Quaker spiritual guide Sandra Cronk speaks with wisdom about "one of the most powerful pathways in the journey to God . . . the time of stripping and emptiness called by many 'the dark night.'" Cronk is careful to distinguish this dark-night experience from the sense of the divine absence experienced by those who lose sight of God through negligence or who have not yet become aware of God's call in the whole of their lives: "The dark night describes the situation of those who have had a growing sense of relationship with God and are suddenly bereft of God's presence, direction and consolation." Usually, our response is to try and fill the void with old or new kinds of prayer and activities, to pressure God, as it were, to return. But none of these efforts will work. There is only emptiness.

Often a form of the dark-night experience may accompany a depression or bereavement. But it is important to distinguish this essentially spiritual process from a clinical illness. Identifiable hormonal imbalance or manic-depressive mood swings and evidence of severe, repressed anger or resentment and suicidal thoughts—these require skilled medical or psychological help. But sometimes, along with grief or depression, we may be invited to undergo a re-patterning typical of a dark night. We may move from self-centeredness to God-centeredness, from self- to other-concern.

> Our strivings after meaning and purpose—indeed, after God—have brought us to the end of ourselves and our own ability to encompass God. As we stand at the edge of these limits, we face nothing, or so it seems. But, paradoxically, just at this point when we face nothing, rather than meet ourselves or any other elements of creation, we may encounter our creator. In that empty place, we can at last know that which transcends ourselves. We realize that in our relationship with God in the past we have turned more to God's gifts

than to God alone. We have looked for comfort or challenge. We have looked for direction and meaning. These are fine and good, but now God brings us beyond those divine gifts. We come to God alone. We have, in the past, confused God's gifts with God. Now we begin to move beyond this confusion.

Cronk goes on to describe the profound re-patterning that may begin at this juncture.

> The re-patterning can happen because the old structure of our lives has been broken up. All those good but creaturely pillars will no longer serve as the center of our lives. Now that they are taken away, a new center can emerge. The new center is God. This new center is not simply an intellectually or emotionally based faith in God. The dark night journey has re-shaped our activity patterns, our value system, and our whole being so that God is the functional center of our living. [This] . . . does not demean God's work in the natural world, our relationship with friends and loved ones, or our service and ministry in God's created order. The dark night journey does not take us to a place where we ignore these natural elements of human life. Rather, it allows us to see where we have inappropriately invested our faith, security, and trust in that which is created rather than in the One who underlies all creation. In the stripping of the dark night we encounter God in a deeper way than we may ever have allowed ourselves before.

This sort of dark-night patterning is not necessarily part of every Christian's life, nor is it universally the experience of those who live in families. A lively sense of the joy and gift of the changing cycles of family may be most persons' experience. But both the rhythmic and unpredictable fluctuations of any family unit may open the way for this deep re-patterning. To the extent that we have experienced the

SEASONS OF A FAMILY'S LIFE

touch of grace through our spouses and have lived attentive to the brush of angels' wings through the medium of our children, we may be invited into the empty space where God is unknown through unknowing, as a new intimate loving that is more a prayer of mystery than an answer to prayer.

Lent, Seattle, 1999

As I enter the darkened chapel and my eyes become accustomed to the dawn light, I see, sitting in the pew ahead, a young Methodist clergyman and his wife who, the retreat group has been made aware, is in the third month of their first pregnancy. Our presider calls us to prayer and we begin our morning praise. "New birth" is the overarching theme of this Lenten retreat, and we reflect together on the mysterious way in which God's life grows inside us. The rest of the retreat attendees are older or, if younger, single and childless. I find it delightfully fitting, in the context of spiritual reflections on the way God makes all things new, to be sitting behind this young woman at prayer as, feeling lightheaded and queasy, she lets her head rest on the pew in front of her while the rest of us stand. I have loved watching her be first in line in the dining hall all week, carrying her tray with its two full glasses of milk and its carefully considered supply of protein; loved observing the worried solicitations of her young husband as the ancient yet ever-new drama of burgeoning life is played out now, with the two of them as the central characters.

It is through the stuff of our own ordinary experiences, especially the experiences of family, that we become aware, by analogy, of the extraordinary truths of faith. The new birth proclaimed in the gospels is, among the many things it is understood to be in Christian communities, a radical transformation like the transformation of pregnancy: life turned upside down, life lived from the inside out, life experienced as a mysterious and wondrous energy that remakes and changes us, life intensely and irreversibly linked to a life other than our own.

It is over a decade since I was pregnant. Thus I find myself less in the shoes of the young Methodist wife for whom the numinous adventure of new life has opened up as though for the first time in the history of the world than in the season of relinquishment and awareness of the rhythms of endtimes.

Part of this has to do with children leaving the nest or straining to burst beyond the nest's safe edges. It also has to do with a newly defined relationship with my husband's mother who, at age ninety-four, has come to live in a skilled nursing facility ten minutes from our house. This always proper and self-contained woman who had lived an independent single life as a school teacher until age forty and then a life of independent widowhood after age sixty is now dependant on a wheelchair to ambulate and the assistance of virtual strangers to get out of bed, use the restroom, and bathe herself. She and I have had a cordial and respectful relationship over the past twenty-five years, but it was always the shared bond with my husband, her only son, that tied us together. Now uprooted from her hometown and plunged into sudden physical dependency, I have become the daughter she never had: the one who remembers to phone with news when we can't come by, to alert the nurses when some ailment she is too self-effacing to mention is in need of treatment, to write the letters to church friends left behind, to replenish the Kleenex and the depleted tin of sugar cookies.

I find myself observing the mysterious features of endtimes with as much tenderness, if not as much delight, as I observe the features of new beginnings.

I visit the Omaha nursing facility at mealtime. I am told that Bob had a run-in with the floor. "And the floor won," he notes wryly. The discolored gauze bandage on his forehead and the rust-colored stains decorating his polo shirt are evidence of the encounter. Bob has laboriously pulled his wheelchair up to the table where I am temporarily seated. Bob is one of the tablemates in the dining hall where my mother-in-law, June, now routinely takes her meals. On my right, I am flanked by Bob's wheelchair; June's is on my left. She has turned to Judith, on her left, and is inquiring whether the tea planned for next Sunday, which the two have just mentioned, will be held here, in this "church." Experts in aging and memory have informed me that the nouns are the first to go—first the proper ones, then the common. "Yes, here, in the restaurant," Judith informs her, craning her neck and one good ear in June's direction. Bob, determinedly wrestling open the lips of a milk carton with his one useable hand, clarifies for me, "Here, in the dining facility."

The facility is large and light-filled and decorated in the pastel color scheme ubiquitous to nursing care facilities. Lavender tablecloths and wallpaper borders flecked with tiny pink hearts provide cheer. Dried-flower wall displays create a country kitchen atmosphere.

Fred, the fourth tablemate, has just been rolled up to the table in a movable chaise bed, his feet swathed in white sheets, permanently raised above the level of his head. The chaise is maneuvered sideways along the table and a hospital tray fitted across his chest. The aide, a large silent girl of American Indian extraction, shifts Fred's water glass and silverware off the lavender table onto the tray with a languid gesture.

My mother-in-law, a woman who for the first ninety-three years of her life was the picture of fastidiousness, has collected a small nest of spaghetti strings in her lap. They escape, unnoticed, between tremulous fork prongs on the excruciatingly long journey across the cantilevered divide between plate and lips. Now nested, they leave a pale red trace of sauce that spreads on her shirt like a halo about the nest.

This is a place of endtimes. A place where the tough spiritual arts of surrender and gratitude are no longer idealistic virtues but lessons hard-learned. To be part of a family is to enter into the fullness of human life, not only as a social, biological, and psychological adventure but as a spiritual one. To find God present in all things is the thrust of the adventure. To explore the human face of love in family is to probe the contours of divine love itself.

Each phase of this journey of family life has been rich with spiritual lessons in forgiveness, gratitude, detachment, compassion, unconditional love, discernment, attentiveness, humility—the list is endless. It has given flesh to those lovely but ethereal concepts that are sung with such abandon: "I surrender all," "Let us break bread together." But the greatest part of the discipline has been to continue to allow family life to genuinely become sacramental, to allow it to be the visible entryway into the invisible mystery that surrounds and undergirds all life. The spiritual art is to remain attentive—among the piles of cast-off clothing in a teenaged bedroom and the withered limbs of wheelchair occupants, as well as among the blooming cheeks of pregnancy—to the grace of the present moment, to the presence of God.

Chapter 9

JUSTICE AND MERCY SHALL MEET

The Countercultural Arts of Family Life

The world would be better off
if people tried to become better,
and people would become better
if they stopped trying to become better off.
For when everyone tries to become
better off
nobody is better off.
But when everyone tries to become better
everyone is better off.
—PETER MAURIN

They mill about the classroom exchanging quips; bright bursts of laughter punctuate their conversations. They are nervous, these students in my Senior Theology Seminar, for today they will appear before the faculty and present as formal readings their carefully researched term papers on the topic, "What Is Christian Holiness?" They are nervous about the questions they may be asked. The first reader is one of the more garrulous in the group, a truly thoughtful young man with a great sense of humor. He has worn a flannel jester's cap to class and impishly asks me if I think it goes well with the gray suit he has donned for this academic rite of passage. For his holy mentor, my student has chosen Daniel Berrigan, the contemporary Jesuit priest and nonviolent activist who, along with his brother Philip, was for a time on the FBI's "Most Wanted" list. The atrocities of the Vietnam War had galvanized the brothers into action. Their Christian consciences pricked by reports of napalmed children, the Berrigans began a campaign of civil disobedience to awaken U.S. churches to the hard truths of war. For their nonviolent, prophetic actions they were frequently jailed; they used their prison time to serve as unofficial chaplains to fellow prisoners. My student, looking uncharacteristically formal in a gray buttoned-down shirt, delivers his paper passionately. He is clearly moved by Berrigan's unflinching Christian opposition to the "works of war." Other students have presented well on a host of holy mentors—Teresa of Avila, Teilhard de Chardin, Anselm of Canterbury, and Martin Luther, among others—but few of the presentations have been so provocative and delivered with such élan.

One section of his paper deals with Berrigan's critique of the American family. Too often, the Jesuit activist complained, young idealistic Christians abandon their vision once they take on the responsibilities of childrearing. Caught in the relentless cycles of consumer culture, families succumb to the forces of self-interest and material acquisition and, in the Jesuit's analysis, unthinkingly become a part of the societal pressures that contribute to poverty and thus violence and even war. In the seat next to me sits my student's fiancée, her short straight brunette bob a striking contrast to her betrothed's blond curly mop. She is enormously proud as she senses the lively response in the lecture room to his presentation.

It is to the "critique of family" section that the faculty questioner returns after the completion of the reading and the burst of enthusiastic audience applause. The faculty member's specialty is foundational moral theology, and he queries my student about the theological sources of Berrigan's views but circles around finally to the family question. "What about someone who, say, has twin boys? How does he balance social conscience with the responsibilities of raising these boys?" The class twitters because they have seen the professor's identical tow-headed toddlers in the halls of the Theology Department on a late Friday afternoon when their dad has popped in to pick up student papers on his way home. Glancing fondly at his fiancée seated next to me, my student admits that he has to wrestle with this question as well, that it's a live issue for him, too. He goes on to explain that of course not all Christian families lack social conscience but that perhaps prophetic witness that puts one behind bars for years might not be the favored choice for the parents of small children. Yet families do have to take seriously the challenges of the gospel in ways that might seem at times countercultural.

I empathize with both my colleague and my student, for we too have struggled over the years to know what it might mean to live faithfully what the Christian tradition has long called the "works of mercy." The imperative to social responsibility has appeared under a number of other names in history, notably "the social gospel" or the "option for the poor." But I rather like the ancient designation and the way in which it has been illuminated over the years. The works of mercy are two-fold, both corporal and spiritual, and the list reads this way:

> To feed the hungry
> To give drink to the thirsty
> To clothe the naked
> To harbor the stranger
> To visit the sick
> To ransom the captives
> To bury the dead
> To instruct the ignorant
> To counsel the doubtful
> To admonish sinners
> To bear wrongs patiently
> To forgive offenses willingly
> To comfort the sorrowful
> To pray for the living and the dead

The works of mercy have scriptural roots and were traditionally seen as an obligatory response to the command that we do unto others as we would have them do to us. As a virtue, mercy is distinguished from charity in that it is related to justice (as charity is not necessarily) because it concerns relationships between people. In our contemporary and rather impoverished American conception of charity, which consists basically in voluntary (tax-deductible) giving of one's excess to those less fortunate, there is little sense of genuine mercy or of the empathetic discernment of misery involuntarily suffered by another. Nor is there much sense of justice or the conviction that wealth is first and foremost a gift to be stewarded for the benefit of the common good.

As thin as our secular conceptions might be, I am certain it is enjoined on Christians, and thus Christian families, to take seriously the implications of the injunction "love your neighbor as yourself." Clearly, someone like Daniel Berrigan, as a celibate member of a religious order, has a certain freedom to witness God's justice and mercy in ways not everyone feels able to do. It is not true, however, that families are exempt from some practice of the works of mercy; nor have families been completely co-opted in the way Berrigan bemoans. I think of the Evangelical Sojourners Ministry in Washington, D.C., which describes itself as "a Christian ministry whose mission is to proclaim and practice the biblical call to integrate renewal and social justice" and publishes a magazine, runs a homeless shelter, teaches, organizes public witness, and promotes service. Sojourners and other groups (local and national) provide opportunities for families to be actively involved in reshaping our society in response to the divine imperative for justice and mercy.

As my student rambled through his response to the faculty questioner, he finally hit upon what seemed to him the most adequate response to the question, How does one balance social responsibility with the task of providing for one's own children? "Teach your children well," he asserted. "Teach them well."

Although in general I feel that I have been more profoundly formed by my children than they have been by me and that the deepest spiritual lessons of my life have been acquired in the course of parenting, it is of course true that we are crucial agents in our children's spiritual formation. One essential way I believe we form them is by offering an alternative vision to the one that our society provides. Most religious communities offer their adherents a challenge to our secularized materialistic culture. Christian denominations and groups within denominations have variously defined what in Christianity is countercultural. We may disagree about reproductive and sexual ethics, about the relationship between church and state or the church and capitalism, about military service and the proliferation of arms, about the death penalty and criminal justice, or about the role of women in church and family. But as divisive as current issues might be, the energy around them speaks to the inherently countercultural thrust of the Christian vision.

For on the starlit pastures of Judea on a night so long ago, the human community was invited to embrace the "news of great joy" (Luke 2:10). A child was born who grew in wisdom to manhood and who inaugurated his public ministry in the synagogue in Nazareth by reading from the scroll of the prophet Isaiah, affirming that this prophet's words were fulfilled as he spoke.

> The Spirit of the LORD is upon me,
>   because he has anointed me
>   to bring glad tidings to the poor.
> He has sent me to proclaim liberty to captives
>   and recovery of sight to the blind,
>   to let the oppressed go free,
> and to proclaim a year acceptable to the LORD.
> [Luke 4:18–19]

From the earliest years, this prophetic vision of a transformed world has been understood within diverse Christian communities, not only as eschatological hope or a metaphor for personal salvation but as a vision for which the church (Christ's body) longs and into which it lives. Thus the corporal and spiritual works of mercy or variants of them become central to the authentic Christian life. There are hundreds of contemporary expressions of mercy that have emerged from the churches, and church youth groups regularly get involved. Each family must search its own soul and ask in what ways it has lived the countercultural arts of the Christian life.

Santiago, Dominican Republic, March 1998

We are sandwiched, thigh overlapping damp thigh, between an elderly *campesina* who precariously balances a pyramid of plastic grocery satchels on her ample lap and the wiry *guagua* conductor who perches adroitly on the two-inch strip of vinyl seat not occupied by my husband. Sixteen of us at the moment are pressed into this dilapidated van that hurtles in ninety-degree tropical heat along *Calle Duarte* toward the center of town. The *guagua* jerks suddenly to a stop alongside a pink concrete block *pharmaceria;* the *campesina* indicates that this is her stop, and we clamber out for a moment into the bright sunlight. Then we squeeze into the crowded van again with two additional passengers folding themselves accordion-style next to us, urged by the agile ministrations of the conductor who now, until the next stop, hangs outside the opened sliding door, his long dark hair streaming back in the wind and looking for all the world like an ancient Aztec warrior.

On the corner bench behind us, our fourteen-year-old daughter, damp bangs plastered to her forehead, tries to fit her nose into the thin triangular window to catch a breath of air. Jostled and tossed as the *guagua* bounces over the pot-holed, pockmarked roads, we do not speak. The rattling of the old van vies with the blaring rhythms of the *Bachatta* pulsing from the radio speakers. Suddenly, the driver utters a high-pitched "Aye-yah!" and swerves to avoid a heavily laden donkey and its owner, who amble into the busy thoroughfare. Our twelve-year-old son, straddled on a wood crate just behind the gearshift, yelps and clutches the seat back next to him.

As we pass through the busy commercial section of Santiago, the crowd in the *guagua* gradually thins out. When we arrive at *Calle Americo,* the last stop before the *guagua* will turn around to reverse its route, we can be counted a mere handful. We unfold our stiff limbs and descend, pausing to reaccustom ourselves to the novelty of standing still, then head up the street to our destination, Hogar Luby (Luby's Home). It is 8 A.M.

Friday morning is our designated time to volunteer at this hostel for the orphaned, disabled children of the poorest of the poor. Perhaps *orphaned* is not the right term, for some of the children are visited regularly by a parent. But in this economically hard-pressed region of the world where public services are scarce and skeletal, the severely challenged child of a family that cannot survive without the labor of every member cannot be kept at home. Thus Hogar Luby—an understaffed, crowded, repository for infants and children of every imaginable disability, some of whom will grow to young adulthood here. We have chosen this service site over several others. The program of which we are a part is sponsored by our university back home, and my husband and I, with our two youngest in tow, have traveled to the Dominican Republic as faculty members, with sixteen college students, for a semester immersion in the Third World. Some of our pre-med students have chosen rural hospital placements, and the education majors have volunteered at local elementary and preschools. We could have chosen to work in the state senior center, in the *bateys* (those squatter camps of the Haitian sugar-field migrants), or with the omnipresent street children who magically appear, soapy sponge in hand, alongside automobiles when traffic slows or who accost you in the city parks waving their shoe polish and offering to shine your shoes for a *peso*. But we chose Hogar Luby because it was a site where we could volunteer together, where Spanish proficiency was not a requirement, and where the work could be done as ably by a twelve-year-old as by someone just turned fifty.

Our first visit to Hogar Luby had left us stunned and choking back tears. The hospice houses perhaps forty children in three small rooms on the second level of a cement building in the middle of a crowded city block. There are no screens or panes on the few windows, and flies move freely in and out. Half-eaten bowls of porridge lie about, uncollected by the two or three poorly paid women who try to feed, bathe, and dress these forty souls—some bedridden, many incontinent, some withdrawn, others belligerent and noncooperative. There are the hard cases—the twins with something like cystic fibrosis (we are told they are seven years old), each of whom weighs perhaps twelve pounds; they lie kitty-corner from each other all day long in their shared crib, emitting an acrid odor no matter how often they are bathed. There is also the sweet-faced, perfectly formed little boy—Gaudi we call him—who returns our attention with a dazzling smile yet who at one year is unable to sit or hold up his head. We see blindness, paralysis, autism, undiagnosable seizures, Down's syndrome, multiple sclerosis, deafness, deformations of every conceivable kind. We leave after our first visit to Hogar Luby shaken.

But each week as we return, the disabilities of the children fade to peripheral consciousness and their particular charms come into full view. Twenty-year-old Maria claps excitedly when we first arrive and rushes over to lay her head on a shoulder. Young Jose is bright and responsive and hindered only by his inability to walk. Both Maria and Jose flourish on the little outings we take to the nearby city park, each of us either carrying an infant, negotiating a wheelchair, or holding a resident firmly by each hand. Our daughter loves the infants' room where she can feed, bathe, and dress one of the dozen or so tiny persons in the cribs that line up along the walls and crowd the middle of the room. Our playful son enjoys the open area where those residents who are already dressed, mainly boys from perhaps six to twelve (it's hard to tell ages here), gather. He brings a ball and paper party hats, which are a great hit.

Friday visits to Hogar Luby are only a part of this semester's lessons for our family and our students. We have studied Caribbean politics, sociology, history, and religion. We have traveled to the mountain *campos,* to the *Zona Francas* and the urban *barrios,* to the Haitian *bateys,* to Haiti itself for Holy Week where we walked the Good Friday Stations of the Cross along the route where the blood of the martyrs shed in the struggle for Haitian self-government was still fresh on the stones and in the people's memory.

Our presence here in the Dominican Republic is as much for us as for the people we have come to serve. It is less about giving to others than about realigning our own vision, about coming to see ourselves in these "strangers," coming to acknowledge as family those it is all too easy to dismiss as "other."

When our eldest daughter was young and we lived in Santa Barbara, my husband worked for a hunger relief organization that worked along the U.S.-Mexico border. Her childhood memories include not only the beauty of the Southern California coastline but the squalor of the squatter communities in the Tijuana dump. Our younger two came to childhood consciousness later in Nebraska where my husband and I hold university positions. Famous for being "a great place to raise a family," Omaha has been good for us in many ways, but it is culturally and economically homogeneous. As our youngest grew, it felt as though, despite us, they remained shut off from any real experience of the larger world in which they live. When the opportunity to serve as the semester faculty on the *Semestre Dominican* and to take our daughter and son came along, we jumped at the chance.

For each of our children now, "the poor" are not remote or anonymous; they have names and intrinsic dignity and are known to be very much a part of a shared world. They are Vittorino, a gregarious *campesino* whose coffee harvest, like all the harvests here, has suffered from an infestation of worms. They are handsome Arturo, who dances so beautifully and works in maintenance at the Santiago center where we stay—Arturo, who earns less in a year than our daughter makes in a month back in the states working Saturday mornings answering the phone at the school switchboard. And there is Juana, who is dying from liver cancer in her one-room shack in the barrio, solicitously attended to by her husband of thirty years who loves her more than life itself. These are the faces of our children's world.

Chapter 10

THE BELOVED COMMUNITY

Reconciliation

Give us each day
our daily bread
And forgive us our sins,
for we ourselves
forgive everyone in debt to us.
—Luke 11:3–4 (Jerusalem Bible)

This morning I left the house with a bad taste in my mouth. In the great scheme of things the encounter probably mattered little, but it rankled and put a sour, early spin on my day. I had been swiftly moving through my morning routine, had washed my cereal bowl, thrown a load of wet laundry in the dryer, and was blow-drying my damp hair when I suddenly realized that our high-school-aged son had not appeared. Often he is out the door, headed to a study session, before I'm fully dressed. Long ago he took full responsibility for his own awakening. This morning the clock read 6:55 A.M., well beyond the time he usually rises. Quickly, I opened the door to the attic loft he calls his own and shouted up the darkened stairwell. His low grunt and the rustle of sheets were the first sounds that came from above; then a yelp and an angry expletive rang out. His tall, tousled body seemed to catapult to the second floor. I retreated to my own bedroom to avoid the flurry, but he was angry about sleeping in and let me know it. I managed to remark, as he stormed out and slammed the front door, that perhaps I was not the best person on whom to take out his frustration.

During the day, the angry incident receded in consciousness as meetings, classes, and e-mails took over. By the time I arrived home that evening, I had mentally placed it aside. When our son arrived home and entered the kitchen where I was boiling water for pasta, my first thought was not of the morning. But when he turned to me and said, "I'm sorry about this morning. It wasn't your fault. It was mine," the earlier pain surfaced. Yet it immediately dissipated. His simple yet heartfelt apology meant the world.

A survey of Catholic lay ministers conducted within the last decade or so indicates that, in the opinion of those who minister to families, the central spiritual dynamic of family life is forgiveness. In the intimate community of family, it is inevitable that we hurt one another. It is inevitable that we reach the limits of our endurance, our patience, our acceptance. It is inevitable that we disagree and challenge one another. The breaches created in the bonds that bind us must constantly be healed. We must return to one another again and again, to ask for forgiveness, to offer it, to accept being forgiven.

I have often felt that the central mystery of Easter is the one that is revealed in the post-resurrection story recorded in the gospel of John. The disciples are gathered together in a closed room, and Jesus appears with the greeting, "Peace be with you." The account is most often remembered as the story of Doubting Thomas, who put his finger in wonder into Jesus' wounded side. But that is not the heart of the story. The significance of the account is found in breath—in Jesus' breathing on the disciples and announcing,

> Receive the holy Spirit
> Whose sins you forgive
> are forgiven them
> and whose sins you retain
> are retained. [John 20:22–23]

This passage has been understood in the Catholic tradition as the institution of the sacrament of reconciliation. But it clearly speaks as well to the power that we all have to transform our relationships through the spiritual art of forgiveness. We have a radical power to either free or hold each other captive. We have the capacity to open ourselves to God's peace. I do not glibly suggest that forgiveness is easy. Nor do I say in cases of abuse or genuine wrongdoing that "it's all right" is an appropriate response. Quite the contrary. Forgiveness is often a long, demanding process that involves truth telling, justifiable anger, or an appropriate action to redress wrongdoing. It may come only long after an intervention or after many years of healing work. In a recent book, Flora Slosson Wuellner, whose ministry is spiritual renewal and inner healing, interprets the beatitudes found in the gospel of Matthew as outlining a process of forgiveness. In her reading, Poverty of Spirit becomes facing our hurt and naming our need; Mourning means making space for pain, grief, and anger; Meekness translates into the embrace of God's gentle power; Hunger and Thirst for Righteousness equals release to new healing choices; Mercy becomes seeing the wounds of those who wound us; Purity of Heart translates into focus on God's light; Peacemaking remains just that—peacemaking; Persecution for Righteousness is explored as living whole among the unreconciled. This leads to "forgiveness fully formed" in which God's power is able to flow to, in, and through us, releasing us from the burden of revenge and resentment, fear and shame.

Wuellner is speaking here of a profound process of transformation, one that may seem too grand to undertake. But in the context of family life, especially in its day-to-day ordinariness, forgiveness is in fact a central healing art that strengthens, deepens, and makes our love broader and more generous. It is a spiritual art of the first magnitude. It is part of what, I believe, all Christians are called to, part of what we are enjoined to be as followers of Jesus who, in his Sermon on the Mount, defined for us the shape of our lives. "Blessed are the peacemakers" (Matthew 5:9), he is remembered as saying, as well as "love your enemies and pray for those who persecute you" (5:44). When he taught his followers to pray, he required that they implore, "forgive us our debts, as we have forgiven those who are in debt to us" (6:12).

These scripture admonitions to peacemaking, love of enemies, and forgiveness are not identical but they are intertwined and are part of a greater theme—that of reconciliation. Reconciliation is the final bringing together of all things, the meeting of opposites in a profoundly creative manner. Reconciliation involves the healing of quarrels, the resolution of differences. The word, quite literally, means to "make friendly."

A reconciled community is a community of friends, a world transformed. Such an expansive vision of a world of genuine friendship sustains most of the religious traditions across the globe. It is echoed in the haunting promises of the Israelite prophet Isaiah of a Holy Mountain on which the lion and lamb lie down together and harm and ruin will be no more. It is heard as well in the angel's proclamation of peace at the time of Jesus' birth, as recorded in the gospel of Luke. It is lodged in the Islamic message of the Ummah— the community of universal harmony. It is discovered in our national consciousness, in the prophetic imagery of Martin Luther King Jr., who longed for "The Beloved Community" in which the violent scourge of racism would no longer divide sisters and brothers.

Reconciliation includes the promise of a true and lasting peace. This promise corresponds to a longing that lies deep in the human heart. Such peace is not simply the absence of conflict but a more substantive reality. Peace in the family has everything to do with the greeting Jesus gave to his disciplines in that closed room two millennia ago. His breath was enspiriting. It conferred the Spirit that would bind them together. Through their mutual forgiveness, they would become a genuine community, not of isolated individuals coexisting in a state of armed truce but a communion that shares one life because each member is animated by the vital energy of the Spirit. No longer closed in on themselves, each is an open vessel into which and out of which the Spirit flows. The authentic life of this community would only be realized when the "in-betweenness" of their separate selves was acknowledged and acted upon. These disciples could thus *be* the church.

The family has been called the domestic church, the smallest yet absolutely essential unit of the gathered church. The domestic church is the intimate community called to live out the mysteries of faith, hope, love, and forgiveness, just as, on a wider scale, the gathered church is called. No domestic church is conflict-free. Nor is the gathered church for that matter! Indeed, healthy conflict is a natural component of any human community, and it is essential for growth. Creative conflicts provide us with the opportunity to work through our differences and learn from them. But our overarching concern should be to work toward the realization of community as envisioned in the gospels. (In case this seems too noble a description of the family, we should remember that "the church" is not some monolithic and ideal body but a collection of fragile, broken, sometimes heroic and always expansively dreaming people not too different from the ordinary family.) A Spirit-filled community is not an impossible ideal but a promised reality. What is necessary for it to be realized is for us to begin to disarm our hearts. For our hearts are the place where that inflowing of Spirit is transformed into the Spirit's outward motion. Whatever constricts our hearts, whatever arms them and erects barriers around them, impedes the action of the Spirit, which is the vital life-substance of genuine community.

Omaha, 1987

I am standing, arms crossed in front of me, staring stonily at my eleven-year-old who is burrowed in the corner of an armchair. Her snippy attitude of noncooperation coming at the end of a long, frustrating day has pushed me over the brink. We have become "the enemy" for one another. In my current perception, eleven years worth of similar moments rise to consciousness, forming in my mind a dark history of rudeness and rebellion. At this moment, my daughter is completely defined by this recollection of mine. Her narrowed eyes and firmly set jaw tell me that she sees before her a similarly onerous specter—the "mean mother" met in previous encounters. She lashes out verbally. I counterattack with a scathing comment (quite unpremeditated) that cuts through her defenses and wounds to the quick. I know I've hurt her feelings deeply. Conscience stirs but my anger overrides it. "She's being awful." "Why can't she cooperate?" "She's had everything handed to her on a silver platter, and now look what I get back," I fume to myself.

Sometime later, tempers cooled, I grudgingly say I'm sorry. "I was tired and your attitude was very hard to take at that moment," I say curtly. She shuffles around a similar disclaimer, and we make up—sort of—to go our separate ways.

Later that night, I awake with conscience fully alive. My hurtful comment appears in a different light. Events occurring earlier in the day had left me cross. The comment leveled at her probably carried much of the residual weight from the earlier events. It didn't even belong to her! My comment also belonged to the phantom energy I had created out of my own selective imagination—an impossible child who was "always" contrary. Where had the real memory been? All the countless loving encounters, all the good times shared, all her gestures of affection, all her gifts of self?

And my "making up" seemed, there in the dark bedroom, like self-defensiveness. Had I really "seen" her hurt? Or was my "I'm sorry but . . ." a way of communicating that I thought I had nothing to be sorry for? Was I simply unable to accept my own capacity to inflict harm? Was I too proud to see myself as anything but the perfect mom?

As she dresses for school the next morning, I go and sit at the foot of her bed. This time I genuinely say I'm sorry. I explain why her behavior was aggravating to me, but I also explain that much of my venom didn't properly belong to her. We are reconciled and experience peace.

It is not easy to disarm our hearts of the defenses we have constructed. Naked hearts are vulnerable. Unhealed wounds become exposed. Our own fiercely self-protective and self-aggrandizing motives are uncovered for review. Our prejudices are laid bare. But our faith calls in to allow our hearts to be thus disarmed and naked.

By this I do *not* mean that we are called to experience ourselves as doormats or as worthless or as victims. No. We are called to the full dignity of the children of God and no power, violence, or insult must be allowed to violate that dignity. The sacredness of the human person is the inviolable starting point of our faith. Nor do I mean that at times we, as parents or family members, must not stand firm in our actions, if they are justly motivated, in spite of the protests of our loved ones.

But we must learn to recognize and respect the sacredness in each other as well as in ourselves. To do this, we need to disarm our own hearts. What is it in each of us that keeps our hearts so defensively posed that we are unable to see the sacred dignity, the God-belovedness, of each other? Perhaps it is pride or lack of a sense of self-worth. Perhaps we take our hidden feelings of inadequacy out on our children when they refuse to live up to the exacting standards we would like them to achieve so that we can feel adequate in the eyes of others. Perhaps we subtly downgrade a spouse because he or she does not seem a fitting extension of our own fragile need to be deemed important or socially correct. Perhaps we are locked in a situation of codependency with an alcoholic or substance-abusing family member, believing ourselves somehow at fault, covering up, refusing to believe in our own innate dignity and worth. What are the ways of violence in our own hearts?

Two little gospel admonitions alone could, if we allowed them, occupy us in the arts of peacemaking for the rest of our lives: "Love your neighbor as yourself" and "Love your enemy." They enjoin us first to experience ourselves as deeply beloved by God. Each of us. Just as we are. Treasured. A beloved daughter or son. They then enjoin us to extend that experience to others. To learn to see that each human person is indeed a creation of the divine hand. That "impossible child," those estranged in-laws, the loveless wife or husband—they too are treasured and beloved. We are enjoined to see one another with eyes of love.

Whenever we have an "enemy," we have the opportunity to become bearers of peace, to arouse in ourselves and in the "other" the knowledge of who we truly are. Especially in our own families we can, through the healing of memories and the offering of forgiveness, begin to love those who have become enemies. Are our hearts pliant and strong enough to begin to dismantle the walls that separate us from each other?

To disarm the heart is the work of a lifetime. It begins in those frequent intimate encounters in our own homes: an irritable exchange over the breakfast table, a longstanding feud with an unpleasant aunt or uncle, a clash of wills between parent and adolescent, the dull monotony of a marriage growing cold. We need to look into our hearts to discern the subtle ways we arm them and then begin to dismantle the weaponry there. We may then begin to be transparent enough that the Spirit, the bringer of peace, may find an opening in us into which it can enter and through which its life can be poured out.

Chapter 11

FOR EVERYTHING ITS SEASON

A Meditation Across Time

For everything its season, and for every activity under
   heaven its time:
a time to be born and a time to die;
a time to plant and a time to uproot;
. . .
a time to weep and a time to laugh;
a time for mourning and a time for dancing. . . .
   —Ecclesiastes 3:1–2,4 (New English Bible)

I had arrived at the reception for the speaker immediately following the lecture. A member of our department had arranged for faculty members to meet at his house for cheese and wine and a follow-up discussion of the annual Theology-Philosophy lecture. We were clustered around the Brie and Port du Salut when our host's wife and their two school-aged children trooped in through the kitchen door. Their son still wore the yarmulke that he had donned for the High Holy Day service. The threesome were fresh from celebrating Yom Kippur—the Day of Atonement—that most solemn of Jewish High Holy Days. My colleague's wife plunked herself down on a dining-room chair. Having long since adjusted to the particularity of this mixed-faith family's religious life (he's an active Episcopalian; she and the children are conservative Jews), I was treated to an account of the night's service. "I rarely cry," she admitted, "but tonight at the Kol Nidre (during the prayer of mourning for the dead), I wept buckets. This is such a wonderful season!"

Each religious tradition celebrates its seasons. Often those seasons are related to the natural rhythms of the earth: spring's new beginnings or fall's harvest-tide. The rhythms of the earth—its budding, flowering, and dying—and its hidden growth are part of our mysterious and graced experience of being created beings. Our mindfulness of the particular quality of each natural season and of the transitions between seasons is also a mindfulness of the mystery that sustains creation itself. Thus our sacred celebrations that commemorate nature's changes honor nature's author.

Often our religious celebrations are related to the story of the tradition's founding or significant events in its history: Buddha's birthday, the Muslim Night of Power, the Passover seder that commemorates the exodus of the Israelites from Egypt, the nativity of Jesus, or his death and resurrection to new life that Christians celebrate. Each religious tradition thus has a calendar on which its holy days are observed. These calendars allow practitioners to hallow time in a particular way. They allow the observant person to achieve a heightened awareness of the sacred story the community remembers. The story is, as it were, played out in time once again in the course of the religious year. The Christian liturgical calendar moves believers through an annual cycle that reaches back into cosmic prehistory, anticipates and records the birth of Jesus, follows his earthly ministry, recreates his passion, death, and resurrection, records his post-resurrection appearances and the founding of this church under the inspiration of the Holy Spirit, and looks forward to his final coming. In this annual dramaturgy, we find inscribed both the context and the meaning of our little lives. Living conscious of the unfolding liturgical year, we also weave the story lines of our own personal dramas into the cosmic drama. The church season illuminates the season of life in which we find ourselves, just as our personal experiences give contour to the evolving liturgical year.

For everything there is a season. And for each new season, a new insight is graciously given or hard won.

WINTER

——

Santa Barbara, December 1977

Had I never heard those words before? Surely I had. But on the first Sunday of Advent when, eight-and-a-half-months pregnant, I stood at the ambo in the sanctuary of St. Barbara's Parish and sang the Advent psalm refrain, "You know not when the time is coming," I felt as though all the rich layers of meaning inherent in the season of Christmas preparation were laid bare. Little did I know that the following Wednesday, a full two weeks before the projected delivery date, I would be in labor. "You know not when the time is coming." These are all of a piece: the waiting of my own pregnancy, Mary's waiting, the long-ago waiting of the world for Christ's coming, the waiting that in our war- and sin-scarred world we do for God's final coming, the waiting each of us undergoes each year for God to be born once again as fresh hope in hardened hearts.

Moreover, at any given season of life we are a child, a youth, a bride, a groom, a parent, an aging family member, then an elderly one. As it is with each one of us, so it is with us as families. Each year, as the sacred drama is enacted once again on the stage of the Christian church's seasons, we find ourselves in a new season; we are newlyweds, new mothers, fathers of adolescents, empty-nesters; we are at the graveside of parents—the matriarchs and patriarchs of a clan. The many layers of meaning inherent in the sacred seasons are exposed. The sacred seasons of our own families add rich overtones to the liturgical melodies taking place. And nature's contrapuntal melodies weave in and out of the seasons of the religious calendar, creating a symphony as dense and evocative as any composition by Mahler, Beethoven, or Brahms.

——

For Everything Its Season

She had just turned three early in the month, and it was late for her to be awake. But it was Christmas Eve, and I was singing with the folk group (which shows how many years ago this was!) scheduled for the evening service. She was in the choir loft with us, wedged between open guitar cases, pressing her nose between the thin wooden slats of the loft so that she could watch the pageantry unfolding below. The sanctuary of the Old Mission, with its exotic décor culled from its Spanish and Native American origins, was crowded with banks of vivid red poinsettias. Candles were everywhere, winking slightly as draughts of chill air crept in from the California winter night through transepts and beneath doors.

We were anticipating the end of the liturgy. The priest, as local tradition dictated, would emerge from behind the altar, with the antique statuette of the Christ child cradled against the lace and gold of his vestments, then proceed the length of the aisle and exit out the wide wooden front doors to the life-sized nativity scene set up on the Mission's front lawn. There, warmed by the steaming breath of the live donkey and the wooly presence of three sheep, the child would be laid in a crude manger between the kneeling statuettes of a brown-haired man and a blue-mantled woman—in a manger that, until this night, had remained empty.

We were awaiting the moment. From her perch high above the rest of the congregation, she could make out the movement near the high altar, a press of lace-suited altar boys with tall, lighted tapers flanking the celebrant. But it was not until the procession had come half-way down the aisle that she caught sight of the Christ child. She inhaled quickly and turned and looked to me.

Nearly a quarter of a century later, I recall that look as vividly as if it were yesterday. It was not the look of a little girl who has seen something delightful; it was not even the look of a child who has been anticipating and then receives a marvelous gift. In the air between us that still reverberated from the chords of a carol stretched an inarticulate arc of knowing. It took my breath away.

I suspect that if I had tried to tell her, when she was a teenager, about that moment, she would have rolled her eyes in that archetypal way and sighed wearily about her mother's "poetic moods." I don't know what she would say now—perhaps that her only memories of those early Mission Christmases are of the fragrant fir, festooned with paper, yarn, and gilt ornaments created by the kindergarten religion classes that stood in the west niche of the nave of the church. Occasionally, I wonder if I am remembering accurately or if the heightened emotion at the time colored my perception. Then I recover the moment and simply savor it.

At the time, no words came with the knowing that passed between us. But in retrospect I have been able to supply a few that hint at it. There were layers: the beauty of the liturgy, the specialness of the feast, the first-timeness of so many childhood events. But more distinctly, there was the felt sense of God-with-us. In that three-word phrase was a universe of wonder.

Christmas is the celebration of the birth of Jesus. It is the memorial of an event that took place two millennia ago. It is also the liturgical acknowledgment of the incarnation. It is the feast of God-with-us. For Christians, this means that at a crucial point in history God spoke a Word that ushered humankind into a radical new relationship with the divine. But God-with-us does not end with that historical moment. God-with-us is also the deep grammar of our everyday lives.

I think, in some part of ourselves, we know this. But the knowing is obscured by so much: by the messages of culture that persuade us that "what you see is what you get," by our propensity to become engulfed in our own worries and woes, by the inability of family or friends or community to dream with us beyond our common wounds or quarrels. Yet, in some part of us, we do know that God is with us. We come into this graced awareness most vividly when we experience a life-changing event. All of us who are parents will recognize the unspeakable wonder felt at the birth of a child. The first time you hold that tiny, fragile person, you are ushered into an almost terrifying sense of the mystery of the life that is beginning to unfold under your protection. There is no experience quite like being ushered into a darkened nursery by new parents to gaze, with them, on their sleeping infant. It has all the solemnity and joyfulness of prayer.

It was Saint Francis of Assisi, known to many today mainly as the "birdbath saint," who introduced us to the practice of celebrating the Feast of the Incarnation by placing a baby in a manger. He was in the Italian town of Greccio on the Feast of the Nativity in the year 1223 and was grieved that so little was being made of this extraordinary day. Francis was overwhelmed with the thought that God had come to us in poverty and helplessness as a tiny child. For Francis, poverty was the key to understanding how God both was and is with us. To be a Christian was, in his eyes, to imitate the poor man Jesus who, born naked in a rude stable, died naked on a rude cross. Francis lived poverty in a literal and spiritual way. He owned no property, held no prestigious position, acquired no great learning. He identified with the suffering of the humble and marginalized, as well as with the suffering of Christ. In midlife, weary from the administrative conflicts in which his followers were embroiled, he sought rest in the little town of Greccio. Wishing to reflect, in his distinctive and theatrical way, on the nature of the child whose birth was celebrated that night, Francis arranged for a crude stable with live animals and a newborn child to be set up in the hermitage where he was staying. He wanted to see with his own eyes the poverty of Jesus—the poor man who lived among us. He wanted to stand by the cradle and see God-with-us. And he wanted to live it.

The poverty of the babe in the manger is realized in us when we have hearts simple and naked enough to be touched and changed by an encounter with love. If we have eyes and hearts open not only during the Christmas season but all during the year, we too might see and realize God-with-us in the vulnerability of the children who are given to us to protect and tend, in the love made visible between spouses, in the sustaining relationships of friends, in the faces of the poor, in the cries of those in need, in the ordinary fabric of the created world.

When she was three, my daughter's favorite Christmas carol was "Away in a Manger." We used to sing it together at bedtime in the Christmas season, gathering up the images of the little Lord Jesus, his sweet head resting on the hay, sheltered by the beneficent gaze of the starry sky, and surrounded by lowing cattle. The carol's second verse ends with the singer's plea, "Stay by my cradle." The Christmas crib, the darkened nurseries in our own homes, the cradles of the poor—these are the privileged places of this season of incarnation, the places we are invited to stay and to wonder and to have our breath taken away.

SPRING

—

The string quartet has finished its rendition of a Mozart piece, and the four young performers smile into the warmth of the polite applause of families and school friends. As they return to their seats at the round tables set with pastel, floral place settings for the school's annual mother-daughter brunch, my daughter turns to me and lifts her eyebrows—her sign that she is somewhat less than impressed with the amateur rendition to which we have just been treated. She is here, I know, partly because her friends are and partly because she knows I cherish these events. Given the option, no doubt she'd rather be sleeping in on this Sunday morning. "I'm starving," she hisses into my ear, then settles back, knowing she must wait patiently for the Mass to conclude before she can dive into the sumptuous buffet laid out on side tables for the occasion by the country club staff.

The presiding priest makes note of his all-female, temporary congregation, then proceeds to address the on-again-off-again relationship he has observed between his own sister and her high-school-aged daughter. He demonstrates the off-again rhythm of their relationship by holding up his hands, each of them clutched tight. Then he turns his hands over and opens them, forming two fleshy vessels.

> If you leave your hands open and are willing to give away everything, you also will be able to receive all the new gifts that come your way. If you hold on to things, the past, grudges, anger, resentment, and so forth, you not only will not give, you will be unable to receive what is offered.

I look at my own hands folded together in my lap. The image is moving and apropos. With this daughter, I have done a lot of cling-

ing and holding on. Yet in years past, this has not been the way I graciously moved into life. I'd like to open my hands more generously
now, without fear of being burnt or hurt or having everything taken
way. I'd like to remember that I can be open to receive the gift and
grace of what comes next. I turn my hands palm up and cup them to
form two fleshy vessels.

SUMMER

Northwest Wisconsin, Monday, August 8

This morning I am awakened by the cry of the loons piercing the mist. I pull back the eyelet curtains framing the windows above the bed and hoist myself up, chin resting on the sill. The damp scents of the wooded lakeside slip in to meet me with the morning fog. I have been told that, as a species, loons are sixty million years old. So their ancient cry connects my hearing with the early Cenozoic era when woolly mammoths and saber-toothed cats could have roamed these shores.

We arrived too late last night at the cabin to have a visual sense of our surroundings, so I feast on this scene with first-time eyes. Big Doctor Lake is shallow, wide, and virtually uninhabited; this morning it is a gray, still-looking glass, framed in pines. Its beauty is unquestionable yet modest compared to our usual vacation view of the Rockies' dramatic grandeur, but there is a gentle quality to the landscape that invites introspection. Lakewater laps the edges of the boat dock. In the still dawn air, the rhythm of my breath is at first a counterpoint to the lapping. Then the two sounds converge, breath and lake water, in and out, back and forth.

I slip on jeans and sweatshirt and wander outside, leaving spouse and children still asleep. Peering through the fog, I try to spot the loons. Thoughts from the spirituality conference of the past weekend surface. The precise and gentle inflection of one speaker's voice comes back. The seventy-year-old monastic spoke on the art of living—a "wisdom" talk that held the participants in rapt attention for two hours. Asked a year ago to reflect on the topic, she had spent the intervening months ripening in the rich loam of monastic silence. Of the sixteen "virtues" of grace-filled aging she named, I recall especially the first three: remembrance and its two companions, forgiveness and gratitude.

Remembering is primary to the art of living, she said, especially as one lives long. As we look back over the fabric of our lives and take stock, the task first becomes one of loving our true story. It has made us what we are. All of it—the moments we wince at, the battles we lost, the disappointments, the delights and triumphs—these constitute our unique history. It is precisely there that God finds us and that we find God. My husband's favorite quip, "Scars make a body more interesting," and writer Maya Angelou's remark, "I wouldn't trade anything for my story now," float into consciousness.

I locate the loons against the tapestry of lakeside forest: two of them, an inseparable couple, gliding noiselessly, then dipping and submerging only to appear at the far side of the lake long minutes later—a glide and dip practiced for sixty million years.

"The art of remembering," the monastic said, "is practiced by threading our way between the two temptations of remorse and nostalgia." As we review our lives, it is tempting to lapse into bitter regret. Remorse is bred when we are unable to embrace our entire story, when we cannot gratefully gather up the episodes and the memories and cradle them, when we cannot forgive ourselves and others. Some memories sting too much or do not conform to our ideal images of ourselves. To embrace them, we need hearts gentled enough by the realistic experience of both our own deep goodness and real limitations. I think gingerly of the memories I hold close, obscured from my own constant awareness as well as from others' view. Do I dare to let them in, to claim them as the mysterious path that has helped bring me to where I am now? Can I risk knowing myself with genuine humility, not blaming, not disclaiming, but really seeing with clear and loving eyes?

The speaker's presence emerges into retrospective view: the soft white wisps of hair circling her face, the precision of her choice of words, the unassuming stance that nonetheless communicates dignity, the sense of genuine self-worth born of realistic self-knowledge.

Tuesday, August 9

I have taken a brisk midmorning walk and discovered the nearby town of Siren; there's a "business district" a block long, with another

For Everything Its Season

perpendicular stretch of several blocks along the nearby highway; two taxidermy shops; one grocery store, and an abandoned, weather-beaten structure with the words "Hotel Siren" painted on one side. Photographs dated 1911 hung on the walls of the Main Street Café, tell me that this was once a lively resort. Hotel Siren was at its hub.

Besides remorse, the other temptation to steer clear of in this artful business of remembering is nostalgia. It is too easy to live in a romanticized past, "lending strange charms to truth" as our conference speaker phrased it. The art comes in remaining connected to our past without falsifying or tidying it up. On the plane out, earlier in the week, I had been reading a thin, compelling book on women's autobiographies. What struck me was the author's contention that until quite recently (with the poetry of a group of women writers, including May Sarton, Ann Sexton, and Sylvia Plath), women tended to write in the old genre of female autobiography—a genre that tends to find beauty in pain and transforms rage into spiritual acceptance—a genre in which the very real anger, passion, or despair that is the stuff of life is not revealed. How much of my remembering as a woman, both as a writer and as a spiritual seeker, has been shaped by the narrative restraints of female autobiography? What the author was suggesting was not that women should adopt a let-it-all-hang-out, encounter-group attitude in the remembering of their stories but that they should steer clear of the temptation to romanticize the past. I wonder how much of the "spiritual reflection" that I do is hindsight romanticizing. Or is it, in fact, the belated recognition of grace present in what has seemed to be far from God? Do I unwittingly succumb to the temptation of nostalgia in this way?

Wednesday, August 10

The red wooden cabin has been in our friend's family for some time. It houses a thousand memories—in the photos and drawings on the living-room wall (of a multigenerational family reunion, a youngster proudly displaying a foot-long catch, the cabin socked in by snow-drifts); in the cedar chest with its assorted board games; in the shed with its cords of wood, horseshoes, dart board, barbecue grill, life-jackets, and canoe paddles; in the antique crib and rocking chair tucked in the corner of the main bedroom.

In the welcome, unfamiliar spaciousness of an unscheduled morning, I stand over the cabin-size stove tending a batch of buckwheat pancakes. My thoughts wander back to my undergraduate studies in history, to my first reading of St. Augustine's *Confessions*. This, at least as I have pieced together the narrative, was the event that launched my adult spiritual quest. At the time, it was the rhapsodic longing of Augustine's prose that captivated me, the anguished prayer that was his life that pulsed off the page. In intervening years, I have taught the *Confessions* and have learned that it is a book of memory. Written in midlife, the *Confessions* is a chronicle of the North African saint's journey from childhood through his conversion to Christianity in his thirty-second year. Along the way, the reader is compelled by the story of his youthful education in the classical tradition, his intense yet complex relationship with his devout mother, his early peer-driven "crimes," his ambivalent attachment to women, including the lower-class mistress who bore his son, his zealous pursuit of life's meaning through his affiliation with the religious sect of the Manichees, his scrutiny of neo-Platonic philosophy and, finally, his exploration of and conversion to Christianity.

Always the probing, restless thinker, Augustine sifts through the artifacts of his personal history to find there the insistent action of God, drawing him closer through events that, in the happening, seemed to have little to do with divine presence. For the North African, the art of remembering is not photographic recall; it is a creative, instructive, and formative undertaking. He comes to know and love God through the evidence of God-with-him in the concrete particularities of his personal history.

On another level, the *Confessions* is a remembering of a vaster kind. As Augustine crafts the narrative of his life from hindsight, he creates an almost archetypal Christian portrait of the human person's movement into God. The inner dynamic of the story shows the young Augustine acting first out of an attitude of *superbia* (pride or self-centeredness) and gradually coming to embrace a posture of *humilitas* (humility or God-centeredness). The boy Augustine is motivated by a grasping ambition to possess wealth, status, love, even spiritual wisdom. His gradual conversion involves learning to let go, to become a recipient, to cease using "the beautiful things of this world" for his own narrow purposes. He redirects desire to the source of beauty—God. Augustine, in so remembering his story, remembers as well the overarching story of Christianity in which the central archetypal figure, Jesus, is one who gains his true life by losing it, who empties himself to become the one who embodies the God-centered life for all humankind. So the *Confessions* weaves together the great and little stories of Christ and the saint with the threads of personal and communal memory.

Thursday, August 11

The wooden bench at the end of the boat dock is warm as I sit. The afternoon sun's presence lingers here, despite a chill breeze skimming across the water from the north. To the west, dozens of white dots are visible on the far shore of the lake. A hundred lotus blossoms close their white-petalled arms above a green sea of lily pads as day's light wanes.

This is our first family vacation without our eldest daughter. A summer job back in the city and the compelling companionship of peers have made the natural transition a reality. Today my husband noted that we took the first of our "nature vacations" with her before the younger two children were born. So she had one they didn't have. I see her, aged four, bent over the homemade valentines her oh-so-earnest mother is helping her make for her preschool classmates. Lace-paper doilies and scarlet foil clippings litter the floor. Behind her, the floor-length picture window frames a late-January view of Rosarita Beach in northern Mexico. Last evening, here in Wisconsin, the four of us roasted marshmallows over a bonfire by the lakeside, my son watching with delight as flames transformed his treat into an oozing mass of black cinders. His valentines this year were the cartoon, store-bought variety, a sign of his loving but working mother's limited time and energy. In Rosarita Beach, we had combed the Mexican markets to find marshmallows to roast in the fireplace of our beach cottage. The ones we found were not white but shades of pastel and would not turn a toasty brown over a fire. They merely melted, sliding off their skewers onto the nearest shoe or floorboard. Memories of valentines and marshmallows link the span of time that arches over our "family nature vacations."

Aging graciously asks us to practice the art of remembrance. For remembrance to yield its gracious fruits, the monastic speaker contends, it must be accompanied by forgiveness and gratitude. Between remorse and nostalgia is the path of embracing all that has been with love. Go back over it all, let go of past pain. Cultivate the patient necessity of freeing ourselves and others through forgiveness. Chip gently away at the hard edges of ourselves that cannot accept that we or others could have done such-and-such a thing. Come to know ourselves as capable of all of it, yet also capable of being transformed in and through all of it. Be grateful for it all. The lovely and the unlovable. It is your story. Claim it with joy.

I wonder if Augustine ever did that—claimed it all with joy. Gratitude he had, overflowing to excess. Yet it sometimes feels as though his gratitude was primarily felt for being rescued from his history, his very human story. How subtle yet profound the difference: to be thankful for being rescued from your past or to be thankful precisely *for* your past. For from it your present, and God-with-it, comes.

Friday, August 12

At dusk we take the canoe out onto Big Doctor. The sky is cloudless, and the water acts like a still mirror reflecting the stands of trees circling the lake. Pines seem to sprout both ways, up and down, rooted in the thin line that is the shore. Our middle daughter spots the loon couple on the south shore, and we paddle noiselessly in their direction. As we come within ten yards of them, they dip down one after the other and disappear. Long minutes later, they resurface and we turn our canoe to follow slowly in their wake.

People remember places. The reverse is true as well. Places remember people. They wear on each other the imprint of their coming together. I carry with me the scent, feel, and spirit of this modest

For Everything Its Season

place, breathtaking in its utter simplicity. My scent, my feel, and my spirit too in some way are carried in the floorboards of the red cabin and the lapping waters at the edges of the boat dock where we tie our canoe.

How rich the strands of memory that converge in this present, this place. How many the threads of story woven together in this now: the loons, with their primordial cry present here for millions of years; the scents and spirits imprinted in the lakeside; the turn-of-the-century tales of the town of Siren; the pulsing prayers of Saint Augustine, born of his excursion, in memory, into his own past; the wide, overarching narrative of the Christian tradition, which has formed and informed generations of believers; the women writers speaking from the pain as well as the beauty of their experience; the fruits of monastic contemplation picked at the end of a lifetime of prayer at a spirituality conference; the stories of the little red cabin and the family whose changing life is recorded in the stuff left in its comings and goings year after year; the changing story of my family with its legacy of nature vacations; my own personal history, remembered best with a love forged from forgiveness and gratitude that sees God active there.

Remembering is a creative, formative venture, not photographic recall. My past shapes my present, but my present remembering also shapes my past. How I claim it—graciously, with forgiveness and gratitude, or not so graciously, with bitter nostalgia or remorse—is important. All these memories have given the present moment the shape it has now. They are the stuff of God-with-me, the places, times, and events, once present tense, that have changed, challenged, and invited me to experience the simple truth that God meets me here. Not where I think I ought to be. Not where I once was. Not where I might some day be. But in my story. Here. As I am. Now.

SEASONS OF A FAMILY'S LIFE

AUTUMN AGAIN

He found the poem in a discarded notebook as he was taking out the trash, one presumably written during a dull moment during geometry or health class, her thoughts wandering along with her gaze out the classroom window, as mine used to so many years ago. I clip the page out carefully, entrust it to the serenity of my dressing-table drawer rather than to the chaotic clutter of the office closet where irregular stacks of cardboard cartons serve as long-term "temporary" containers for the mounds of trip souvenirs, photos (in albums and loose), trophies, recital programs, plastic-encased baby teeth, and locks of hair. I clip the poem carefully and sit with it. Sit with time. Its passing. Our passing. What we pass on to one another. I sit with this.

> bruised hands
> tremble without control
> my grandma
> epitome of dignity and pride
> is dying
> caged in pain
> like a sad bluebird
> long arms so familiar
> change before my young eyes
> into wrinkled bones and dust
> my grandma is dying
> What color were your eyes?
> What color are mine?
> grandma
> my name
> my family

my link to history before myself
her hair used to be done
in pink curlers
her flowered housedress
and capable shoes
jewelry boxes of my childhood
fake flowers
tin marbles
will be all that's left behind
grandma
I want to know
about your farm
and your family
and your life
teach me in your quiet way
but she cannot speak
and she is shamed
by immodesty and mess
fed through tubes
and breathing fake air
just to stay alive
when she has nothing
except
us
to live for
my grandma june is dying
and I cannot say goodbye
because I have not said hello
[elizabeth june]

WINTER AGAIN

———

It was a cool August afternoon in the densely wooded mountainside of rural North Carolina. I had wandered on the fog-shrouded road perhaps two miles from the Moravian Retreat center where I was directing a spirituality retreat for an ecumenical group of Christians. An occasional modest wood home, flanked by a generous vegetable garden, passed me by. The odd dog, doing its canine duty by barking at my approach, sent its warning echoing across the shallow valley through which I walked. Just short of the Blue Ridge Parkway, where the country road ended, a wooden signboard emerged from the fog: "Connie and David's Christmas Tree Farm: Featuring Frazer Firs."

And there they were: sentinels on the roadside, a towering row of Frazers, their evenly spaced limbs heavy with moist blue-green needles. For the past decade, our children and I have chosen Frazer firs as our Christmas tree of choice. When we first discovered them at the local nursery, they were not an obvious choice. After all, my sensate memories of childhood Christmases were intimately tied to the scent of pine wafting through the house and the prickly feel of long, soft pine needles pulled back as ornaments slid onto branches. It took a while, but Frazers did become our tree of choice. Now each year we declare that this one tree, silhouetted against our Omaha living room window, is *the* most beautiful tree ever.

Christmas is a time of traditions. For us that means the Frazer fir and the ritual of unpacking the cardboard boxes that disclose our fanciful, random collection of decorations: Life-Saver and pipe-cleaner snowmen, fashioned in preschool classrooms; tin angels, each with an engraved name under the inscription "Baby's First Christmas"; south-of-the-border straw donkeys and stars, purchased on a

---

135

trip to San Antonio; colorful bread-dough figurines from Bolivia; the plastic ballet dancer, tiny golf clubs, metal art palette, miniature Christmas carol booklet, and basketball-playing Santa that represent our family's various interests; a blown-glass nativity scene hanging from a silver wire; cardboard quotations salvaged from a long-ago Advent calendar. Each year the rediscoveries elicit cries of delight and nostalgic memories of Christmases past.

The eve of the holy day also means, for us, the tradition of five o'clock Mass, followed by dinner at the Indian Oven (one of the few fine restaurants remaining open that evening), and the next day's dawn scramble down to the laden tree. First, we empty the stockings, with their predictable new toothbrushes, tangerines, packs of gum, tubes of hand lotion, or sticks of incense. Then the cornucopia of presents is opened, each one in turn while the entire family watches, comments, and passes around the new book, the cardigan sweater set, the carton of jams and jellies, next-year calendars, exotic bath oils, and new computer accessories.

The Christmas season is filled with the deliciously familiar activities that distinguish our family celebration. When we enter into them anew each year, we are prompted to be mindful of our family-ness, of the rich history of joy, struggle, sorrow, and delight that we have lived together. The remark of a family therapist I heard long ago has stayed with me: severely dysfunctional families lack the rituals, patterns, and traditions that ordinary families reenact in the course of their lives. These patterns provide a family with coherence, meaning, and identity. It is those patterns, unremarkable though they might be, that both express and give substance to our shared life.

The annual re-entry into the season also makes us mindful of the mysterious and wonderful reality of God's coming to us, both once long ago and today, in the ordinary fabric of our daily lives. Our three otherwise oh-so-sophisticated young-adult children gathered once more in the early morning around the tree, eager for surprise and wonder, never fail to touch me. At how many critical junctures, at how many milestones have I been aware of the gratuitousness of grace, of a reserve of love and courage that came not from me but through me and blessed these three young people? And how I feel the

136

SEASONS OF A FAMILY'S LIFE

gracious presence there of those who shared so many celebrations— my father, my husband's father—those who now are gone but never forgotten—God-with-us in the faces, hands, and hearts of those we have been given.

For most of us, the re-enactment of these Christmas rituals stirs up feelings of tenderness and hope: the fragile infant nestled in the manger; eager kindergartners balancing glittering wire haloes on their heads; the succulent fragrance of roast turkey and stuffing; the strains of haunting melodies—"O come, o come Emmanuel"; "Silent night, holy night, all is calm, all is bright"; "Joy to the world the Lord is come, let earth receive her king." God is with us, lit by the rays of a guiding star and heralded by trumpeting angels. New birth. New beginnings.

Yet for all its brilliance and sweetness, there is a darker, more somber side of the Christmas season. Hidden beneath the tinsel and colorful wrappings is the keen awareness of all the ways in which our families, communities, and world fail to realize the promise of Christmas. Violence. Fear. Loss. Betrayal. Despair. This shadow side of the season is all too evident. What is "not yet" stands out in high relief against the backdrop of the bright season. For some, Christmas is just too painful a holiday even to acknowledge. Those of us who are so pained may have experienced too much disappointment, had too many hopes dashed, endured too profound a loss to suffer the promise of the season, at least this year.

Sometimes I think that our frantic American celebration of Christmas—our consumption-crazed compulsive festiveness—stems not simply from our failure to honor the silent mystery so palpable during the season but from a denial of the solemn contrasts that the Christmas light illumines in the darkness of our personal and communal world. And I wonder, with some hesitation, why it is that our bursts of generous giving and our attentiveness to the poor and marginalized, so evident at the beginning of the church year, fade away at the beginning of the secular calendar year. Is it because we see, for a brief time, what God-with-us might mean? Or is it because for an instant we see all too clearly the absence of God? And what happens to our seeing the rest of the year?

For Everything Its Season

The light of Christmas illumines for us the poignant recognition that this sweet moment we celebrate is only the beginning of the story. The long-ago child became a man who suffered and died at the hands of those who opposed the vision he offered. And even though he continues to come to us again and again, always he meets resistance; there is suffering and death. At the foot of the manger, we find ourselves only a side-step removed from the foot of the cross.

When our children were young, the buffet in the dining room always displayed three Advent calendars during the weeks before Christmas. One was always tastefully elegant, one a little sentimental and covered with glitter, and one cheerfully bright-colored. They represented the choices and tastes of our three offspring. Of course, when our three were young, these glitter-and-tissue-paper calendars helped fill the seemingly endless waiting ("How much longer before Christmas?"). And the daily Bible verses we uncovered or the pictured scenes of the ancient story helped to underscore that the waiting was not simply for presents but for the presence of God. Perhaps most significantly, the calendars marked off the specialness of that waiting time. It was a time to get ready, to anticipate, to savor, to wonder, to live expectantly.

In the homogenized time that is our adult twenty-four-hour-a-day, seven-day-a-week, fifty-two-week-a-year, production-and-consumption world, we have to struggle to set time apart. To make it special. To live expectantly. But I think that is the only way we can become accustomed to the light that is dawning on us during the shortest, darkest days of the year. Somehow we must honor the mystery of the Coming in the silence of our homes and hearts. Somehow we must take time to savor the sweetness of what is promised. Somehow we need to remember that each year we are newly invited into God's ever-deepening presence in our lives. And we are newly welcomed into the radical hope of a rising sun, which comes to shine on everything that languishes in darkness and cowers in the shadow of death. The time of Advent is given to us to prepare. The true preparation occurs not in our baking, housecleaning, or shopping but in our expectant waiting, in our attentiveness to God-with-us in the past, in the present moment, and in the deepest longings of our lives.

Sometime during the second or third week of the Advent season this year, my children and I will make our annual pilgrimage to the local nursery to pick out that perfect Frazer fir and carry it home, strapped to the top of the car. My husband will play his traditionally assigned part in the ritual by undertaking the engineering feat of securing the tree in its shallow metal stand and stringing the bubble lights on the blue-green branches. We will step back and declare that *this* tree, silhouetted against our Omaha living-room window, is *the* most beautiful tree ever. Together we will sing the verses of the ancient Advent hymn:

> O come, O Dayspring from on high
> And cheer us by your drawing nigh;
> Disperse the gloomy clouds of night,
> And death's dark shadow put to flight.

And perhaps, if we have honored the waiting and our eyes have become accustomed to the dawning brightness, we might be more able this year to bear the brightness of the season's beams of Love.

Spring Again

———

The spring thaw this year was welcome—perhaps more so than usual, for the ground had been iced over with banks of congealed gray snow for months on end. First, thin spikes of green poked through the gritty white cover. Then the predictable yet always miraculous harbingers of spring emerged in ordered procession: the low clumps of purple crocus, the bobbing yellow heads of jolly daffodils, the dark-green spikes of iris stalks waiting to burst into riotously colored blooms.

Spring also brought with it a longed-for sense of release. At our house, the young people shed their winter outerwear like butterflies burst from their confining cocoons, leaving the front porch littered with their cast-off garments. At the university where I teach, emboldened young men appeared on the campus walkways in denim cutoffs. Their female counterparts, abandoning their navy and black wardrobes, emerged in pastel pinks and white.

Easter is the liturgical season that Christians in the Northern Hemisphere celebrate in the warming sunlight of spring. Easter is, in part, a celebration of the miracle of renewal and revivification that nature celebrates with such sweet-scented delicacy each year. Hymnody suggests as much: "Now the green blade rises from the buried grain, wheat that in dark earth, many days hath lain . . . love is come again like wheat arising green." With wonder, we celebrate the ever-creative processes of life that sustain our earth and all its creatures.

With the arrival of springtime comes hopefulness. Concerns that darkened our winter hibernation seem to dissolve on an afternoon bike ride in the country or during a Saturday morning spent at the Little League baseball field. This discovery of newness, the sloughing off of the brittle protectiveness that winter engenders in us, is not simply biological. It is spiritual as well. How much I identify with Brother Lawrence, the seventeenth-century spiritual guide whose little book *The Practice of the Presence of God* distills such common-sense wisdom. At the age of eighteen, the young French peasant experienced a conversion. Seeing in winter "a tree stripped of its leaves and considering that within a little time the leaves would be renewed, and after that the flowers and fruit appear, he received a high view of the providence and power of God."

This "providence and power of God" is everywhere written on the green carpet of the earth in spring. It is written in the hope felt that renewal is upon us, that chill and dreary landscapes give way to new growth. It is written in our heart as well, as we pray in music the responsorial for the Easter Sunday Mass: *This is the day the LORD has made; let us rejoice in it and be glad* (Psalms 118:24). We repeat the same delighted sentiment in the words of another psalm when we proclaim throughout the Easter season, *Shout joyfully to God, all you on earth* (Psalm 66:1).

Springtime in an agricultural region like Nebraska is obviously a time of new life. Lambs are born, cows calve, and bunnies are everywhere darting beneath low shrubs. We do not need the commercial reminders of plush violet rabbits and fuzzy yellow chicks displayed in store windows to know that new birth is a present possibility, no matter how frozen life seemed in the wintertime just past. In part, Eastertide is a celebration of the power and providence of God the Creator, whose good earth contains within itself the seeds of newness and hope.

But Easter is much more than this. It is not only the joyous recognition of divine creativity but the awestruck acknowledgment of God's capacity to offer hope where none exists, to bring life where death has to all appearances triumphed. This is a much more difficult truth to celebrate than the flowered sweetness of spring. It is a truth that confounds our logic and confuses our sense of the expected course of things. The joyful Easter morning liturgy that is celebrated each year is preceded by the solemn liturgy of Good Friday and the great Easter Vigil on the evening of Holy Saturday.

On Good Friday death swallows up hope. Christians follow Jesus—God's own sign to us that we are beloved children—on the painful road to the cross. God's promised reign on earth dies; the dust of human hope mingles with the blood that pours from his wounds. To all appearances there is no possibility of reversal. Death is not the temporary cold of winter. Death is the final end—of promise, of life, of hope.

On Saturday we find ourselves in the barren landscape of the tomb. For most of us, as for the early disciples, the place is too terrible. We flee. We shrink back in fear. Or if we are foolish enough or enough in love that we cannot believe what our eyes tell us is true, we come, like the women mute with grief, to the tomb to enact the ancient ritual of burial, the anointing of the dead. We come without hope to visit the place where our deepest and fondest hope has died.

Then comes the dawning realization. The heavy stone that sealed off hope has been rolled way. The tomb is empty. The shrouds that were love's confinement have been cast off, tossed away. The impossible is possible. We cry out with newborn life. Easter is the celebration of God's raising Jesus from the dead. As such, it is the celebration that love is stronger than death, that the hope for which our heart was created is not some distant fantasy but an unimaginable promise kept. Despite appearances to the contrary, ordinary logic is defied.

I do not find it helpful to think of the mystery of Easter as a sort of mystery act that God performed to save us from ourselves, defying the laws of nature in the process. Rather, Easter seems to me to be discovered first closer to home, in the heart. Each of us has an intimation of what life should be. We all dream of love truly realized between parents and children, husband and wife, family and friends. We all dream of a world free from hunger and violence. Too often we ignore this intimation until some tragedy or close call jolts us to attention. When we lose a loved one or when violence strikes close to home, we are startled out of our ordinary complacency. It is there, in loss and hopelessness, that the radical hope of Easter is found.

The testimony of the earliest Christians gives us some insight into this radical hope. In second-century North Africa, Christians were persecuted. Two young women—Perpetua, a well-to-do Roman wife and new mother, and Felicity, a pregnant slave girl—became so captivated by the Christian proclamation that a new, transformed era was dawning that they were baptized, despite the risk of death. The account of their martyrdom in a Roman amphitheater has been passed down to us over the generations. In the account, the two women go fearlessly to their fatal encounter with wild beasts. They live boldly in the hope that their new faith proclaims: that both the evil of the world and the power of death and sorrow have been transcended through the resurrection of Christ. For these early converts, this mystery was not simply a matter of belief; it was a reality experienced as present and working in the world. Thus, when she cried out while giving birth prematurely, Felicity countered her jailers' jeers about her upcoming contest with the beasts with the assertion, "Now I suffer by myself, but then another will suffer with me."

When we read the narrative of Perpetua and Felicity's martyrdom in theology class, my students often complain that the story seems so gruesome. The young women seem to glorify death. The students prefer a Christianity that celebrates the goodness of earth and human relationships. I agree to the extent that suffering pursued for its own limited sake is not necessarily redemptive. But too often students miss the hope to which the martyrs' acts point: a radical hope for an utterly transformed world in which love's kingdom is triumphant and in which death and sorrow, war and hatred, misery and pain, are no more.

———

We have lived in the same house for fourteen years now and have shared the joys and sorrows of the neighbors who have lived as long or longer on either side of us. Two years ago, we answered a knock and found our neighbor to the north standing ashen-faced in the doorway. He brought the tragic news about the second daughter of our neighbors to the south. She had been expected home for her younger sister's bridal shower on the weekend following Saint Patrick's Day, but she and another young woman had been found burned almost beyond recognition in an abandoned apartment a state away.

For Everything Its Season

A terrible grief gripped the neighborhood and the parish to which many in the neighborhood belonged. As the gruesome story unfolded in the papers, we learned of the two women's random and separate disappearances from a Saint Patrick's Day party and of a shadowy stranger who had been camping out in the vacant apartment. We learned all these things, although we did not want to have to know, did not want the terrible truth to belong to our neighborhood life. We did not want to have to weigh this tragedy against the hopes we all held for our own and one another's children.

At the funeral liturgy, we prayed the hope we have as heirs to our faith—that death is not the final victor, that love will once again spring green. The witness of our neighbors, whose grief was raw but who have learned slowly, through the care of others and through their own faithfulness, to trust a deeper story than the one life has played out for them, has been a sign to us that Easter's promise is alive among us.

A radical hope is born at times like these—a hope closer perhaps to the hope of the ancient martyrs than to the hopefulness of spring's warming arrival. This is a fierce and hard-won hope—that death will not sever the bonds of love, that loss of one another here does not mean loss forever. It is a hope that does not dwell in the shadow of death but seeks forgiveness and healing. It is a hope that has been cauterized in the flames of grief and doubt and learns to trust in a generous love that operates beyond appearances. This is a hope that rises out of the ashes to move forward with courage into new life.

I have never much cared for the raw cold of winters on the Midwestern plains. Several years ago, however, a young woman of Chinese ancestry in one of my classes enabled me to appreciate the hope that winter can bring to birth in us. She had come to love winter, she wrote in a reflection paper, because in that cold, dreary season, plants send forth their deepest roots. Invisible to all appearances, true and lasting growth takes place deep under the frozen, lifeless topsoil. Nature offers us this profound lesson. Christian faith teases us into an even more breathtaking knowing: that beyond expectation, beyond reason, beyond even hope itself, God offers us Easter. Easter is God's promise that now and always we might have generous, hope-filled life.

Easter is a celebration of the power and providence of God the Creator, whose good earth contains the seeds of newness and hope. It is also the celebration of God the Redeemer, who rises up and offers us a radical hope for an utterly transformed world in which love's kingdom is triumphant and death, sorrow, war, hatred, misery, and pain are no more.

SUMMER AGAIN

—

I have seen her frequently when I have walked the dog on a soft summer evening or driven around our shared street corner on my way to or from work. I have seen her standing or kneeling or bending in her garden. Her house is typical in this neighborhood—a white clapboard structure erected at the beginning of the last century: two stories, a roomy, shaded front porch, and what looks from the outside to be a rambling interior. The house is quite ordinary. The garden is extraordinary. It is a celebration of the earth's capacity for bounteousness and beauty.

I have seen her, with all the seriousness of a surgeon preparing to operate, assess the lush tangle of morning-glory vines that cascade from the roof. She moves among the riotous orange and crimson blooms of late-summer flowers with the solicitous care of a kindergarten teacher monitoring her charges. She surveys her fruit-heavy vegetable bed with parental pride. Her bright, burgeoning garden is a joy to behold. Each time I have passed by, whether from the distance of the car or at intimate, dog-walking proximity, I have found myself thinking, "This woman knows how to inhabit a place. This woman knows how to make a home."

Home as a theme for reflection has occupied me lately. Perhaps this is in part because our children are at an age where my husband and I will, before we know it, find ourselves in an empty nest. Perhaps it is also because I am aware of the tension felt in the Christian life in the experience of this earth, both as a place where we encounter God and as a place of exile. To put it another way: we experience God as both with-us and as still-yet-to-come. I suppose I have always known this, but I feel it now in a new and poignant way.

About a decade ago, a wise spiritual mentor said to me, as I was bemoaning the fact that I was having a difficult time feeling at home in the community where we live, "Ah, that's dangerous business, thinking you can find home." I remember at the time being perplexed at his warning. Making a home—creating an environment in which a family can experience something of the goodness and presence of God—has always seemed to me to be a chief call of Christians who have children. I would go further and say that, in my own spiritual itinerary, the theme of home has been a constant and compelling one. Before I converted to Roman Catholicism, I was drawn by the idea that a Catholic could go anywhere in the world, walk into a Mass in progress, and find herself at home. The language might be different, but the Mass itself was the same, and the parish church or cathedral would never belong just to the community gathered there. The local congregation would belong to a wider family that was intimately conjoined. Everywhere a Catholic went would be home. It was that, to me, stunning insight that overrode any other objections I might have had to the Roman Catholic formulation of the Christian faith. And I wanted to give my children the sense of a spiritual home.

I remember as well being almost livid with a well-meaning gentleman when he suggested that our earth, this place we call home, was perhaps in God's mysterious design destined to soon pass away. The context for my outrage was a parish discussion group on the newly published letter from the American Catholic Bishops on war and peace. It was 1983 and our second daughter was in arms; in fact, she was with us at the parish discussion group. The threat of nuclear annihilation was a fear in most people's minds, and the bishops' letter spoke of our responsibility as Christians to wisely steward our country and its policies so that the unspeakable horror of nuclear warfare might never occur. We were all in a bit of a gloomy mood about the possibility of private citizens really effecting public policy, and the gentleman, I suppose to put our helplessness in a larger context, said half to himself and half aloud that perhaps we could do nothing and that the imminent end of life as we knew it was in the providence of God. At his words I felt the fury rise in me. My choler had everything to do with the little girl asleep in my arms who had hardly begun her life. Fine for you to say, I fumed silently—you at the end of your days, childless and resigned! Don't you dare speak those words for this child or for all the children who have yet to play out the dramas of their lives! Don't dismiss the sacred home on which we live so easily!

The experience of our earth, my faith community, and my own family as "home" has been an essential thread, tying together the segments of my own journey. Yet there remains my mentor's warning: don't call any of this home. In a limited sense, I have come to appreciate his warning as I have grown. I've been on the inside of church communities long enough and with enough ecumenical breadth to know that, for the most part, any denomination or congregation is more like a collection of strangers thrown together who may or may not hit it off than like an idealized home. And I've struggled enough with my own extended family to sense that, for the most part, we inhabit the "not-yet" more frequently than the "already." Our deepest home is in God. It is through our families and our churches and the created world that we are taught, formed, oriented to God. They are thus infinitely important. We have, in a real sense, no other way to go to God than through the ordinary fabric of our lives. But our families and our churches and the earth itself are not God.

Which brings me back to my neighborhood gardener. My soft-summer-night visitation to her blooms and bowers reminds me of the passionate intensity with which we might and must cultivate our lives. Our families, our communities, our earth are rightly the place of our tender ministrations, our constant bending and kneeling, our pruning and fretting and stewarding and unabashed appreciation of the beauty and bounteousness of life itself. We must make a genuine home here. Yet this beautiful, bountiful life does not ease our deepest longing for a home. The restless, unfinished business of the human heart presses at us, leaves us lonely for the not-yet.

I drove rather than walked by my neighbor's garden this past week. She was nowhere to be seen. An unseasonable chill had driven her indoors. Frost had nipped at and blackened all those colorful petals that now folded in on themselves. They hung in limp bunches from beleaguered stems. I had left an empty house (our children who

remain at home tend not to linger but to fly off to their various desti-
nations). And I wondered when I would walk this way again. Early
Tuesday morning, my husband had found the silent body of our
sweet, elderly dog, my walking companion for the past decade, stiff
inside her kennel. It seemed at the moment impossible to ever walk
this particular path again without her.

I know. This is the way of seasons. I know. The frost will be followed by sleet and snow and then, miraculously, impossibly, thin
green fingers of newness will impose their insistent wills upon a stiff,
frozen earth. I will watch in wonder when this greenness refuses to
submit to winter's funereal tones. I will inhabit the place that is mine
to call home with passion and solicitous care. I will watch our neighborhood gardener emerge in her faded overalls and stained canvas
gloves and begin her primal spring rituals of tending, mulching, seeding, and weeding. I will know that she is an image of how to make a
home. I will also feel the primal pull of a homecoming I will never
feel here.

Autumn Again

––

The colors are at their height: scarlet, rust, neon yellow, burgundy, and brown; they spread a canopy of motley over the lush, green expanse of campus lawns. Even the undergraduate students clad in sweat pants, having just rolled out of bed on their way to 8 A.M. classes, have to admit the colors are stunning. I have walked the perimeter of the eight-hundred-acre, rural Pennsylvania campus early this morning and now am encamped in a quiet corner of the university library, dew-damp shoes drying underneath my chair.

> Yet, O Lord, you are our father
>> we are the clay, and you the potter,
>> we are all the work of your hands. [Isaiah 64:7]

Last evening, I had my first glimpse of our middle daughter's freshman dorm room—walls plastered with posters, the tiny refrigerator stocked with midnight snacks, the wooden bunk-beds placed there by my husband, who had traveled with her across the country and had helped her and her roommate during orientation two months ago. Her roommate, blond ponytail struggling free from its elastic, breezed in from dance team practice, breathless with co-ed enthusiasm. I commented appreciatively on their housecleaning efforts, launched in honor of my arrival: throw rug vacuumed, clothes hung up in neat rows in the curtained closet. Later in the evening, after a guided tour of the campus by night and with a quick stop at the ballet studio to check on tomorrow's rehearsal schedule, we paused at the door of her red-brick residence hall. Our hesitation recorded the strange newness of the changing relationship felt between us. "How amazing," I managed to say. "All your life, you've lived in my home; now I am visiting yours." Her eyes teared up, and we held each other for a long wordless moment before we kissed goodnight.

> For he knows how we are formed,
>   remembers that we are dust. [Psalm 103:14]

Fall's fiery colors presage winter's bleak landscape and its dreary chill. Today, the two eye-level windows placed in this library corner straight ahead and to my right function as Shinto torii shrines framing the breathtaking beauty of orange and russet poplars that, in serpentine fashion, line the central campus mall. Often in the past, the onset of the chill weather has saddened me, plunged me into psychic hibernation. But time has gradually inscribed on my heart the knowledge that winter, for all its surface bleakness, is for the vegetative world a time of intense creativity. Although barren to the human eye, trees in winter experience their greatest root growth. Their life force reaches out, plunges deep, and roots into the sustaining soil with its hidden ground waters. So it is for us as well.

> You formed my inmost being,
>   you knit me in my mother's womb. [Psalm 139:13]

Life, if we let it, forms us. It teaches us the varied wisdom of its seasons: the mysterious arts of welcoming our children, of becoming the nurturers, the active protectors and teachers; then it teaches the arts of letting go, of loving more, of having hearts stretch wide and deep enough to surrender—the fiery brilliance of our autumn harvest yielding to the gray yet deeply rooted wintertide.

> The LORD God formed man out of the clay of the ground
> and blew into his nostrils the breath of life,
> and so man became a living being. [Genesis 2:7]

Dry yellow leaves have begun to accumulate beneath the trees; mostly they lightly pepper the still-verdant lawns, scattered by the first

For Everything Its Season

gusts of autumn air. I wait by the entrance to the library for my daughter to emerge from her English composition class. Soon we will share a last lunch; then I will be off to the airport and home. A long-ago landscape comes unbidden to mind: Encinitas, Mexico, February 1983. I make my awkward, pregnant way down the sandy slope to the edge of the seashore. Protective of the new life forming inside me, I hold on to the tough vegetation that sprawls from the rock nearby. How many instants like this have there been? Mindful of the life I've been given care of, that is forming, first within me then outside myself under my sheltering protection. How many instructions, kisses, tears wiped, tears shed, wounds bandaged, wounds opened, lessons taught, lessons learned, encouragements, discouragements? How wide an expansion of life and heart? In these eighteen years, how have I formed this daughter? How has she formed me?

A breath of breeze shakes loose a handful of curling rust-colored leaves and sends them cartwheeling across the library lawn. Fashioned from the clay out of which all life forms emerge, we human beings most resemble the creator. We are lovingly molded clay into which the breath of life has been breathed.

For God formed man to be imperishable:
   the image of his own nature he made him. [Wisdom 2:23]

Tech rehearsal. In the stairwell of the theater, five of the dancers are warming up, sweaters slung over shoulders to protect unlimbered muscles. To my left, several rows ahead of me in the theater seats, the young choreographer whose original dance is about to be rehearsed is conferring with the lighting designer about musical cues he must observe for the dance to create its intended effect.

At this college, where the tradition of Christian humanism is taken seriously, the arts are alive. Here the creative life is not viewed as the prerogative of a gifted few, cultivated for the amusement of the well-to-do. Here creativity is seen as an essential component of the fully human life. For dance, music, drama, and the musical arts are pursued not primarily for personal fulfillment but for the sake of the human community fully alive, for the arts draw us deeply into the parts of ourselves where our most urgent questions and desires lodge. These desiring questions have as their source and end, God.

This dance, reminiscent of Romeo and Juliet, tells a story of feuding families and first love. Other compositions by the young choreographers are less narrative in structure, more concerned about the sheer beauty of movement and the kinesthetic capability of human form. Longing in the arch of an arm. Laughter in the twitch of a shoulder blade. Vigor in a leg springing into air.

Darkness descends on the stage. "Cue fourteen," the stage manager's voice prompts the invisible technicians. A circle of pale light appears downstage left to reveal a crouched figure. The first strains of orchestral music rise to greet the ear. Bend and stretch. Whirl and leap. Extend. Contract. Rest. Release. Spring. Pull back. One dancer mirrors another, then breaks away in a surprise parting of ways. The stage is crowded with furtive, darting shapes pulsing to the beat of drums. Then sudden stillness. A lone flute arpeggio accompanies a sinewy body slinking to the floor.

Out of an assemblage of bodies, light, space, and music a unique form emerges. The ordering of sound. The patterning of line. The articulation of rhythm. This dance, both universal and utterly particular, emerges from our human capability. And it is ours precisely because we are created in the divine image and likeness. Perhaps it is in this, our creativity, that we are most like God. Given form, we in turn give form to that which is not-yet.

> I went down to the potter's house and there he was,
> working at the wheel.
> Whenever the object of clay which he was
> making turned out badly in his
> hand, he tried again, making of the
> clay another object of whatever sort he pleased.
> [Jeremiah 18:3–4]

So much of the creator are we that we are capable of fashioning an alternative world in which we become gods, wielding power to create and destroy, to honor and dishonor ourselves, our fellow creatures,

For Everything Its Season

creation itself. Thus we must be refashioned, re-formed, so that our creations will reflect our true identity—shaped by all the available means of grace, including the formative lessons of the seasons of our ordinary lives: the springtimes, summers, autumns, and winters, each with its own wisdom to be gleaned, each with its own shaping hands.

> So too, all men are of clay,
>> for from earth man was formed. [Sirach 33:10]

Humus. That is the etymological root. Humus, earth, clay. Humility, the most central of Christian virtues, is rooted in the earth, in our identity as creatures who have been formed from clay. True humility holds together two impossible truths in its firm grasp: that, astonishingly, we are made in the divine image and likeness and that the divine image in us is obscured, wounded, or marred. The truth of our being is revealed in our recognition of that likeness and limitation. Both blessed and broken. Humility holds these two truths in tension. We are clay with the trees and the grass—life giving, yet soon to wither.

> but we hold this treasure in earthen vessels,
> that the surpassing power may be of God and not from us.
> [2 Corinthians 4:7]

What is the formative lesson of this autumntide of my life? What is it to let the soft clay of my being be re-formed by the process of this second daughter's springtime flowering, her moving away? She was fashioned first inside me, took shape all those years under my nurturing hands. Now I open them wide and let her go—the fruit of this harvest season. What deep roots, stretching into hidden ground waters, will the coming season of winter bring?

> Like clay in the hands of a potter,
>> to be molded according to his pleasure.
> So are men in the hands of their Creator,
>> to be assigned by him their function. [Sirach 33:13]

SEASONS OF A FAMILY'S LIFE

Winter Again

Only twice did I see a tear on her cheek, and both times were during the last year of her life. My husband had never seen her cry. Not that she was an unfeeling woman. Far from it. But she had been groomed in an era when genteel lives were characterized by the privatization of emotion. My mother-in-law did indeed always present herself with great dignity and graciousness. It was a presentation that was consistent, for her demeanor never changed, even when she was by herself. When admiring friends remarked that her tearless countenance at her husband's funeral revealed her great faith, she shook her head ever so slightly and spoke to her son in a muted aside, "It's not faith. It's courage."

Everything about my mother-in-law bespoke life habits of moderation, good sense, and courteous restraint. From the weekly routines of her retirement years (Sunday school and church attendance at First Presbyterian, frequent visits to shut-ins in the local nursing care facility, sometimes a P.E.O., Retired Teachers' Association, or church circle meeting, occasional concert attendance, always an evening of bridge) to her modest and practical purchasing patterns, she was a model of reserve.

Her tastes, by the standards of the fashion world, were frankly middle class, mid-Western, and conservative. We buried her in the navy blue, cotton-and-rayon suit she had kept immaculately cleaned and pressed for two decades. At her throat were the soft flounces of one of her favored white-polyester Sears and Roebuck blouses, preferred because the sleeves were long enough for arms that she considered a wee too long for her otherwise short torso.

The effusive act of weeping would have seemed oddly out of place for my mother-in-law.

Without tears our dried heart could never be softened, nor our soul acquire spiritual humility, and we would not have the force to become humble. [Symeon the New Theologian]

Tears are deemed a gift by many ancient masters of the spiritual tradition—a gift not merely in the sense of something given but in the biblical sense of a charism—a gift of the Spirit, belonging on the list that Paul enunciates in his first letter to the Corinthians. Tears were, for the ancient church, given to some along with wisdom, knowledge, faith, healing, prophecy, and the like, for the life of the entire community.

It seems to have been Athanasius, the great fourth-century bishop of Alexandria, who first spoke of tears as such a gift. But other notable, early Eastern Christian writers expounded on them as well. Assuming that inner dispositions had a corresponding outer expression, the Eastern church writers most often saw tears as the outward manifestation of the spiritual experience of *penthos,* a term we might translate as "compunction," which means, quite literally, "to puncture with." *Penthos* refers to the spiritual pain due not only to a shocked recognition of sin and human weakness but the simultaneous awakening dissatisfaction with sin and longing for God. To have our hearts thus "punctured" is both the beginning and the dynamics of the journey.

Words do not always manage to completely express a thought. Tears always allow us to see the full affection of a soul. [Geoffrey of Vendôme]

Twice, in my presence, a lone tear did escape from my mother-in-law. Both times occurred after we had moved her from her hometown of Manhattan, Kansas, to an Omaha nursing care facility that was a ten-minute drive from us. It was a hard move—one she herself had suggested but that separated her from friends and the familiar scents, sounds, and experiences of ninety-three years. On the first occasion, a Jesuit priest friend of ours, who had met my mother-in-law a number of times during her holiday visits, volunteered to drop in at the nursing facility and perform a blessing. Despite the fact that my mother-in-law's Reformed religious milieu did not include priestly blessings or traditional devotional rituals or the more modern faith-sharing experiences, she seemed open to the Jesuit's visitation.

He had planned a brief prayer and scripture reading that would allow her the opportunity to reflect aloud on the experience of being displaced and give voice to her feelings of loss. The little blessing service assumed a familiarity with ritual practices like confession in which a person's deepest emotions may be readily expressed. Perhaps it was her unfamiliarity with such rituals, perhaps it was her habitual reserve, perhaps it was her failing hearing and sight, but my Jesuit friend found himself having to extemporaneously fill in the silent pauses left empty for her responses. Politely, she listened as he spoke of Ruth and Naomi's itinerancy and of the pilgrimage of all our lives.

When it escaped, he didn't even notice it, nor did he recognize what had occurred when she fumbled for the folded tissue tucked away in her sleeve. One tear inched its way over the deep creases enfolding her right eye.

> Where is the purity of my prayer? The confidence that was in it? Where are the sweet tears instead of these bitter ones? Where is my faith in the shepherd? Where is the result of his prayer for us? It is all lost and gone. [John Climacus]

The ancient East understood there to be different types of tears, some of spiritual origin and import, others not. Spiritual tears in themselves were variously categorized and described. They could have purifying power. They might function differently for those just beginning on the spiritual journey and for those far along. They could be provoked by memory of sin as well as consideration of the goodness of God, the desire for heaven, the fear of hell, or the thought of judgment.

Overwhelmingly, tears were understood as a gracious God-given gift, a wonderful physical sign that the inner world of a person was being transformed. There is in these ancient Eastern masters a sense of the ongoing cleansing taking place as a person draws nearer to God. Tears thus become, in a sense, a sign of the continuing power of the baptismal waters to redeem the created world.

> Baptism washes off those evils that were previously with us, whereas the sins committed after baptism are washed away by tears. The baptism received by us as children we have all defiled, but we cleanse it anew with our tears. If God in His love for the human race had not given us tears, those being saved would be few indeed and hard to find. [John Climacus]

Up through the late medieval era, the Western church continued to plumb its inheritance and to explore the spiritual anatomy of tears. In the early sixth-century monastic rule of Saint Benedict, tears are described as the natural accompaniment of true prayer. And Gregory the Great, whose *Dialogues* in the late sixth century established pastoral practice for generations to come, delightfully imaged the spiritual life as movement through a land sprinkled from below by tears of fear to a land watered from above by tears of desire for and love of God. Wonderfully, the twelfth-century father of Cistercian monasticism, Bernard of Clairvaux, weaving together scriptural images, spoke of tears of penitence as the bread from which one dare not fast for fear of failing in the journey and of tears of devotion, penitence, and neighborly love as the wine that grants spiritual inebriation.

My favorite Western writer who explored the spiritual dynamics of tears is Catherine of Siena. This remarkable fourteenth-century Italian laywoman dominated the spiritual and political landscape of her day. Catherine distinguished tears of death from tears of life and went on to explicate at least four expressions of those living tears. She, like her predecessors, saw tears as the physical expression of a transformative inner process. One changes as one grows closer to God. One changes in every imaginable way. Tears for her thus reflect the degrees and directionality of love at any given point in the spiritual journey.

For Catherine, a disordered heart not yet fixed on God produces tears of death. Such tears arise from some loss and refer more to the pain felt to the self than to any inner growth. These tears make scant reference to God. Tears of life or spiritual tears proper begin with the "puncturing" or "pricking" of the heart. At first such tears are mainly purifying; we weep as we feel sorrow for sins or fear of punishment. Gradually, love erodes fear and we experience the consolation of a loving God. We begin to grow in virtue and feed on God's Word. Tears at this point are prompted both by our hunger for the felt experience of the divine in prayer or with others and by our sorrow when these consoling experiences seem to be withdrawn.

As we grow in union with God, our tears spring more from love of God in God's own self and from compassion for our neighbors. An even deeper stage of union, in Catherine's experience, produces tears of intense gladness and sorrow, sweet tears shed by a heart utterly identified with God's sorrowful, pierced, and infinitely loving heart.

> When the soul grows tearful, weeps, and is filled with tenderness, and all this without having striven for it, then let us run, for the Lord has arrived uninvited and is holding out to us the sponge of loving sorrow, the cool waters of blessed sadness with which to wipe away the record of our sins. Guard those tears like the apple of your eye until they go away, for they have a power greater than anything that comes from our own efforts and our own meditation. [John Climacus]

The second time I witnessed my mother-in-law's tears was at her deathbed. In the manner of many over ninety, she had been felled by pneumonia, then suffered a series of debilitating strokes that robbed her of much of her mental capacity, including the ability to speak and to swallow. Respecting her earlier stated wishes, we refused a feeding tube that would have only prolonged her dying and began the waiting at her bedside. The vigil kept was longer than any of us could have imagined. A frail, birdlike figure nested between the pillows of her hospital bed, her flesh having long ago melted away. Turned gently at regular intervals with as much care as if she had been a porcelain heirloom, she lingered on.

Her dying was to be, among other things, a slow drying. Long since, her veins had collapsed, making the in-flow of intravenous fluids impossible. We kept her cracked, peeling lips and tongue moistened as well as we could, but the water so vital to every cell of the human body could no longer be replenished through her throat or veins. Parched. Dehydrated. More and more a dry, brittle remainder of her former self. How long was it? A week? Ten days? Two weeks? Time was suspended as family, friends, and hospice workers sat, held her hand, prayed, read aloud, and sang. For once, the frantic occupations of our lives were stilled, put in proper perspective as, for a while, all that really matters stood in high relief.

It was then, during what we now know was the penultimate day of her life, that one more tear escaped from my mother-in-law's eye. She could not indicate to us in any way what this tear meant. She could not speak. While her eyes were often open, they did not follow a hand passing before them. She could hear somewhat; that was clear, for her breathing calmed as we sang to her. But an MRI had indicated that the vital blood supply to one entire half and a significant portion of the other half of the brain had been cut off. Ordinary cognition could hardly have been possible.

The day nurse, who knew little of my mother-in-law's history, simply commented, "I can't imagine where that came from. She hasn't received any fluids in a fortnight." The hospice chaplain, presumably in an effort to assure me that the tear was not an indication of pain (which she was otherwise capable of showing but was not doing so at the moment), dismissed it gently. "Probably some nostalgia," he said lightly.

That tear has stayed with me. I prefer not to think of it in terms quite so biological or psychological as either the nurse or chaplain. The memory of it, slipping out onto the dry parchment of her cheek, silences an attempt at explanation. I have no way of knowing its meaning or lack thereof except that on the occasion of my witnessing, my mother-in-law was poised on the edge of utter mystery. And at such a place, spiritual gifts might appropriately be found.

I have told you how tears well up from the heart. The heart gathers them up from its burning desire and holds them out to the eyes. Just as green wood, when it is put into the fire, weeps tears of water in the heat because it is still green (if it were dry it would not weep) so does the heart weep when it is made green again by the renewal of grace, after the desiccating dryness of selfishness has been drawn out of the soul. Thus are fire and tears made one in burning desire. And because desire has no end it cannot be satisfied in this life. Rather, the more it loves, the less it seems to itself to love. So love exerts a holy longing, and with that longing the eyes weep. [Saint Catherine of Siena]

SPRING YET AGAIN

———

My husband and I arrived a bit late, but that was not a breach of etiquette because the invitation was open-ended; the timeframe for the baby shower indicated on the invitation was Sunday, 3:00–5:30 P.M. Nor were we the latest arrivals. Another couple arrived just after we did with their toddlers in tow, still sleepy-eyed from afternoon naps. The unwrapping had already begun, and I slipped into a chair vacated by a colleague who had to leave early to drive her son to a soccer match. The mother-to-be—the wife of a university academic colleague from the Philosophy Department, herself an archivist at the local historical museum—was nestled in a colorful pile of tissue paper and bows, trying valiantly to match gift cards with the packages that lay before her in happy confusion. To my right, an older woman whom I soon learned was the grandmother-to-be was attempting to alleviate her daughter's confusion by scribbling the names of gift-givers on a pad of paper—not an easy task since she had only been introduced this afternoon and was fresh off the plane from Australia!

Over the years, I have become accustomed to the faintly chaotic yet wonderfully generous hospitality of the shower hosts; both are colleagues in the Philosophy Department who work across the hall from my Department of Theology. On Sunday, all of the guests crowded into the old sofas and folding chairs angled around the room, balancing paper plates of potluck finger food on knees, shifting sideways periodically for the stray child compelled by the winsome stuffed animals popping out of gift boxes to dive into the middle of the fray. On the margins of the group, the hosts' teenaged son and his friends grazed briefly at the smorgasbord of goodies, then disappeared into the upper regions of the house. Those gathered were in all stages of the family life cycle. Some were facing soon-to-be empty nests; one couple was recently married; others counted children in the grade or high school years; a divorced colleague's child was half a continent away. All in one way or another were connected to the university community. And all were oohing and aahing as the plush bears, brightly illustrated Mother Goose books, and tiny pastel pieces of apparel emerged from their wrappings.

Looking up from her note taking, the Australian mother began a commentary on the presents she had so carefully packed in her luggage instead of an extra change of clothes. The yellow booties were a gift from her quilting circle. Indeed, the package was addressed not to "Deidre's and Kevin's baby" but to "Diane's Grandchild." The white "comfy" she had crocheted herself from a pattern handed down from their British forebears. The crib quilt of miniscule saved scraps: "Really, it had taken less than twenty hours." But the large quilt of elaborate stitching and complex animal appliqués, suited better for hanging above a crib than for laying in it, she had begun twenty years before. "It seemed like a good time to complete it," she said simply.

Those gathered for the shower read Heidegger, Kant, Chaucer, and Cicero on a regular basis, usually in the original languages, yet when *Pat the Bunny* emerged out of the wrappings, a universal cry of delight went up and everyone wanted the little book passed around so they could flip the pages and rub the fuzzy, bunny-shaped panel of white fabric: "Now YOU pat the bunny!" The father-to-be could not quite grasp what was happening: "Pat the *bunny?*" he laughed. But we were all quite serious. This small cardboard book, for most of us, carried with it the scent and feel of our own young children snuggled close and sleepy on our laps, pushing tiny, fat fingers through a cardboard hole ("Now YOU wear Mommy's ring") and mimicking our words in their soft, sibilant echoes.

Family life is, if nothing else, an immersion in the ever-changing passages of the human life cycle—the fresh beginnings, the youthful milestones reached, the mature transitions of marriage, pregnancy, and childbirth, the "householder" phase with its labors of nurturing, providing, and "world maintenance," the later years of generative wisdom and letting go, the final times of diminishment and death, as well as an immersion in the powerful bonds of love that bind these passages together. Family life is an ongoing celebration of continuity and change. At each of these moments of passage, we are made aware of a deep, often inarticulate awe. It has always struck me as comforting that religious communities offer families ritual moments to mark these ordinary life-cycle events as the sacred times we know they are. Baptism, confirmation, the bar or bat mitzvah, naming ceremonies, the marriage rite, ordination, the funeral—whatever the specific theology that might undergird a rite, the community always blesses the intimate experiences of families with an affirmation of their sacred significance. These ritual moments weave our little stories into the greater Story of infinite significance. They consecrate the care we give to one another.

In several weeks, after their baby is finally placed in their arms and lovingly wrapped in the crocheted comfy knitted by its Australian grandmother, Kevin's and Deirdre's baby will be brought to the baptismal font at First Methodist. There, surrounded by family and friends, it will be welcomed into the community of faith and washed in the waters of life. And those gathered will acknowledge together the infinite and almost inexpressible mystery that lingers in the remembered scent and feel of a child nestled close and sleepy in arms: "Now YOU pat the bunny."

SUMMER YET AGAIN

—

The world is not only a jungle giving evidence of original
sin; it is a garden in which God's kingdom may break forth
through our instrumentality. [Gerald Bednar]

During the years my family and I lived in Santa Barbara, California,
I was privileged to both observe and participate in the creation of a
garden. It was a city park really, but not your ordinary municipal plot
of green. It had no ball field, picnic grounds, swimming facilities, or
structured playgrounds. It was, rather, a plot of land, several square
blocks in size, designed to be a unique garden.

The land originally was the estate of a wealthy woman who
deeded her property to the city when she died. My husband and
young daughter and I lived just a few blocks from the site, and I often
jogged by it. In those years before it was transformed into a public
garden, the property was a wild thicket of foliage bounded by an antique wrought-iron fence. One could see only a short distance into the
mass of native shrubbery and hoary trees.

I say that I participated in the transformation of this tangled
wild wood into a garden—but not because I had anything to do with
its planning or execution. Landscape architects, city planners, professional gardeners, and contractors accomplished its construction. But
as I observed its emergence over many months on my jogging rounds,
I slowly and wonderfully began to participate in the meaning expressed by the garden's evolving contours. The arrangement of the
space itself carried a spiritual weight.

Until it finally was opened to the public, the garden's topography was shielded from full sight. The black fence guarded its secret.
When construction first began, I could see the scaffoldlike arms of

For Everything Its Season

earth movers and hear the growl of heavy machinery as it shoveled and heaved, clearing ground carefully around the majestic trees that were incorporated into the design. Over time, the land was sculpted. Hillocks emerged in one place, deep valleys in another. Nothing in this garden would be straight or level.

If I jogged completely around the property (perhaps four city blocks), I could begin to see the garden's outer edges. Entrance pathways appeared at irregular intervals. Some seemed to meander toward an invisible center. Most branched off in other directions, beckoning to mysterious corners or disappearing over slight knolls. Eventually, the industrial equipment gave way to gardeners' trucks, wheelbarrows, and a forest of tools. Burlap sacks bulging with manure and mulch, rows of plastic pots sprouting seedlings, and an arboretum's supply of plant species lined up inside the fence, waiting to be transported into the as-yet-secret interior of the garden.

By then, the sculpted perimeters of the park were visible from the street. Banks of bougainvillea bushes confettied the south rim with festive scarlet, magenta, and salmon hues. A native oak spread its majestic limbs on the park's west side. Just beyond, I could glimpse a reed-filled marsh. In the distance, partly hidden from view, I could see the upper reaches of a wooden gazebo nestled on the banks of an azure lake.

I remember the morning on my daily jog that I discovered one of the garden's entrances open. The formal civic inaugural was still several weeks away. Nevertheless, the garden beckoned, and I turned in at a slow run. A gravel path led between a spreading bed of dusty miller on the left and a grassy knoll on the right. Soon the path turned, and I was in a small clearing where a wild-rose-bowered trellis shaded a wooden bench, just the right size for two lovers. An alternate path led back around to the right toward a rippling shallow brook crossed by a footbridge, Zenlike in its simplicity. Wild iris caught my eye, their patches of purple contrasting with the gray and black stones lining the brook side. For many mornings I entered the garden, each day from a different direction, always discovering new environments that invited me in. The wide, green hillocks of grass by the small lake called out for family picnics and for children to be running, tumbling, and flying their kites. Oak-shaded benches tucked in out-of-the-way corners invited the solitary reader to retire with a good book. A spiral path up to a rise led the exploring visitor to a bronzed antique sundial. Waterside vistas beckoned water colorists to express creativity with brush and paint.

Even after its public unveiling, when this city park garden was no longer mine alone to explore in early morning, it retained its almost magical sense of unfolding. The garden's carefully choreographed space could accommodate a large number of visitors while still allowing everyone to experience spaciousness, even solitude. The varied elevations, environments, and winding pathways allowed visitors to inhabit simultaneous yet discreet worlds. The garden offered shelter for every mood, every activity, every configuration of persons.

The garden is an evocative symbol in the Christian tradition. It is first found in scripture as an image of God's pristine creation, a place for human beings to enjoy but from which they were cast out. Their alienation was plucked from a fruit tree. So a garden is central in the creation story. It also is central in the story of redemption. It is to the garden of Gethsemane that Jesus repaired on the night of his arrest. A garden serves this time, not as the portal through which humanity passes on its journey away from God but as the portal through which it returns in the person of the crucified and risen Christ.

The garden also appears in the medieval spiritual tradition. There the garden suggests the paradisiacal state of the soul in intimate relationship with its God—restored, through prayer and asceticism, to at least a partial realization of its original nature. I love especially the artistic image, seen occasionally in ancient European churches, of Mary in an enclosed garden. In medieval Christianity, the figure of Mary symbolized many things. She was, of course, the Mother of Jesus. But she was much more. She was (as church councils proclaimed in the fifth century) "Theotokos"—Mother of God. She was identified as the Mother Church itself, as Sophia (God's wisdom), as the Woman Clothed with the Sun of John's Apocalypse (Revelation 12:1). She was seen as the second Eve, just as Jesus was the second Adam. Together with her son, she participated in the momentous

For Everything Its Season

actions of the incarnation and redemption, re-infusing the world with the divine momentum that was its intended course. Mary was the archetype of the contemplative, the one who opens in deep receptivity to the indwelling of God.

Of the many visual representations of Mary as the archetypal contemplative, the Mary of the Enclosed Garden is my favorite. This rendering identifies Mary, the human soul, with the bride of the Song of Songs (4:12) who is likened to a locked garden. Mary, virgin yet fruitful through God's initiative, becomes the symbol of the garden-soul, the fruitful lover of God. Like Mary, we who pledge our deepest troth to God are flowering, fruitful gardens, planted and tended in the intimate enclosure of prayer, letting God's Word and Spirit be the gardener that prunes and nurtures our lives. Mary of the Garden is an image of mystical import: the wondrousness of divine love rooted deep in our heart's soul yields a harvest that is greater than our own power can produce.

A garden is not a wilderness. To encounter the created world in its untamed state, we go to the wilderness. As a geographical destination, the wilderness is a test of physical strength, skill, and endurance. As a spiritual destination, the wilderness brings us face-to-face with our demons, with temptations of the magnitude that Jesus faced when he was sent out to the wilderness, fresh-dripping from his baptism in the Jordan, to be tempted by the devil.

A garden is a "wholly other." It emerges from the happy marriage between the materials of the natural world and intentional human ingenuity. A garden is humanity's dream of an Edenic world: the intentional sculpting of space, the aesthetic arrangement of plantings and vistas, walkways and cul-de-sacs, the variegated colorings of flowers and budding trees, the articulation of mood and meaning. All these are part of the intentionality of a garden, whether it is a formal public garden replete with lime avenues, parterres, and fountains (the English were geniuses at these), or the garden oasis of a private villa (note Italy's splendors), or simply the spring festoon of tulips or crocuses that appear around a modern suburban home. Gardens are testimony to the enduring human effort to fashion paradise from the wilds. So it is with the gardens of our souls.

Bishop Richard Challoner, an eighteenth-century English Catholic spiritual writer, produced a small treatise aptly titled *The Garden of the Soul*. Subtitled *The Manual of Spiritual Exercises and Instructions for Christians Who, Living in the World, Aspire to Devotion,* it was a widely circulated collection of spiritual wisdom, like many that were popular in Europe at the time. In fact, copies of *The Garden of the Soul* found their way to the American colonies and enjoyed a large readership, particularly among the sparse Roman Catholic population throughout the early wilderness years of the young republic.

The book is a guide to the practice of spiritual disciplines that are designed to cultivate the virtues and weed out the vices: the standard ascetic fare of traditional Christian spiritual practice. *The Garden of the Soul* recommends itself to us, not for the uniqueness of its contents but because it underscores the truth that the spiritual life is in great part an intentional life. Like a garden. Initiating and sustaining it, of course, is the grace of God. But spirituality is not simply the untended spirit of humankind; it is humankind prepared, seeded, weeded, fed, watered, and pruned—women and men shaped into something of beauty. The soul becomes a garden.

The wilderness has its own unique, magnificent, fierce beauty that is rightly not subject to our considered designs. But we do have a decided place to play in the cultivation of the world we inhabit and the selves we are. We can let our covetousness, envy, lust (for power and prestige as well as sexual predation), our sloth, anger, gluttony, and pride guide our relationships with each other and the environment. Or we can cultivate the virtues. The traditional Christian list designates seven: faith, hope, love, temperance, fortitude, prudence, and justice. What might our lives look like if they were motivated by our concern to achieve the virtues in our personal and public lives? Perhaps less like the untamed wilds or the asphalt jungle and more like a flowering garden.

The City of Omaha recently began constructing a botanical garden. It is located south of the city center, a short distance from the Union Pacific Railroad yards and a corridor of abandoned brick industrial warehouses, just beyond a neighborhood of modest, aging bungalows. It is an area of town where streets are in need of repair and there still remains a vague flavor of its Eastern European immigrant origins. There is a Bohemian cafe with faded curbside frescoes of Old World scenes. A concrete-block building houses an Italian bakery, founded along with the city itself. Sokol Hall, scene of Polish workers' weekend polkas, now features a random assortment of local and traveling bands. Here city planners at the end of the twentieth century designated space for a garden.

The Omaha botanical garden is a work in progress. I discovered it about two years ago when the only developed areas were the trellised rose garden and the herb plots. We had settled my mother-in-law (for what would turn out to be the last year of her life) in a well-appointed nursing care facility located south of downtown. On my nearly daily drive, I became acquainted with the area and the small green public signs with arrows pointing eastward toward the garden.

The botanical garden is open May through October. This past June was the first time in a year that I had walked through it. Much of the long front drive, past the iron gates that fence it off from the surrounding neighborhood, simply passes by leveled ground. A projected design map gives these barren areas labels like "Japanese gardens," "iris beds," and "nature grasses." In the center of the area is a well-developed rose garden. This June, the dozens of climbing, hybrid, and wild varieties of roses were just past their peak. Blush pink, fiery red, salmon, yellow, and ivory blooms spread themselves wide, their tentacled, pollen-laden centers exposed to the sun.

To the right of the rose trellises winds a path in an oval loop around an undeveloped open area. The path seems to cut a civilized swath on the edge of what is otherwise a tangle of brush, vines, and scraggly low trees. Placed at intervals along the path are wood benches or an occasional gazebo—contemplative resting places for the meanderer. Some of the benches are adorned with plaques memorializing loved ones. A bronze statuette of a startled grazing deer bears an inscription from a surviving spouse. About a third of the way around the arch of the oval, a local funeral home has erected a memorial list in honor of those whom they have buried in the past two

SEASONS OF A FAMILY'S LIFE

years. Running my finger along the tiny rows of engraved letters, I find my mother-in-law's name in the group: June Zirkle Bergman.

To the right of the rose garden is another path. New this year, it leads to an area over the crest of a slight hill. "Bird Sanctuary" the sign reads. I follow the gray asphalt that winds down the slope and find myself in another memorial garden—the gift of a husband to his deceased wife. A wood pergola of oriental suggestion half shelters a shallow pond quivering with black, darting tadpoles. A waist-high wildflower meadow—I recognize the swaying orange poppies, the heavy drooping heads of sunflowers, the purple sprays of lupine—borders the path for a while. Then appears another small pond, a sheltering gazebo, a central clearing with freshly planted saplings, and beds of flowers I don't recognize. Dotting the area are dozens of tall wooden poles on which stand birdhouses filled with varied feed. In the very center towers a tiered martin house.

Why is it that when we want to remember those persons whom we have deeply loved, we turn instinctively to the garden? Perhaps it is because we recognize that in the presence of that mother, daughter, wife, or sister we sensed the presence of beauty so profoundly human it is almost divine. Or that in our relationship with that father, son, husband, or brother we discovered an ordering that allowed freedom, a carefulness that tended growth, an intention that saw and sought the place where love lies.

A garden is a material reminder that Eden is where our story began and where it will end. In our gardens, we fashion our best selves—our creativity bent toward shaping and tending the natural world into a place of graciousness and grace. In our gardens, we remember those with whom we knew that faith, hope, and love are tangible realities and with whom we realized something of the garden that we might be. A garden is an intentional sacred environment, a place where what is most ordinary, human, and earthy gains depth, resonance, and yes, soul.

AUTUMN YET AGAIN

I spent much of September 11, 2001, on the phone to our middle daughter, who is a college student in Pennsylvania, to our eldest daughter, who resides in Los Angeles, and to my mother, who lives two hours north of her on the Pacific Coast. When I wasn't on the phone or in class helping my bewildered students thread their way through the labyrinth of their political and religious questions, I was in contact with my husband, who works at the other end of the university where I teach. We met at the campus noon Mass, which was transformed from an intimate celebration into a standing-room-only assembly of two thousand students, faculty, and staff. Then, after connecting with our sixteen-year-old son, whose Jesuit-run high school had called off afternoon classes to gather the student body in an hour of prayer, my husband and I returned together to campus to participate with our students in an evening interfaith prayer service held on the steps outside the university church. Like nearly everyone in America that day, I reached out first to family members, to those who are closest to me, if not geographically, certainly in heart and mind.

In those first hours, part of me worried that we were not all in close physical proximity. The phone was a blessing, but the habituated gestures of years of comforting or being comforted on a lap or in a tight embrace came back with visceral force. Gradually, as the hours and then days passed, I began to relinquish our daughters and my mother to their geographical distance, a strange replay of the letting go I had done quite recently to send them off to college or to leave home myself so many years ago. One must love more, not less, I reminded myself. I even opened a copy of the book I had written on family spirituality in 1988, soon after we arrived in the mid-West city and moved into the modest turn-of-the-century dwelling where we still reside. Perhaps I needed to recover, in this time of new vulnera-

SEASONS OF A FAMILY'S LIFE

bility, whatever wisdom I had previously wrung from the experience of parenting. I found the section titled "letting go." Yes, it still resonated, although my husband and I have moved much more deeply into the mysterious spiritual lessons of letting go since I wrote the words over a decade ago. In it, I had claimed that letting go does not consist in ceasing to love or detaching oneself from affection but in loving more. This loving more involves radical faith, the kind of faith that trusts that God's presence is available to us, even in suffering and death. The God to whom we look is one who accompanies us in every facet of human experience—a God who laughs, weeps, celebrates, wonders, and is seared with pain just as we are. It is this faith that allows us to let go.

The intimate domestic world of loving care in which we had sheltered our young children had become too small to contain their lives. My own love had to grow. Now, once again, I was called to increase my capacity.

On September 13th, a Jesuit spiritual counselor shared with me a scripture passage from the book of Habakkuk. He had been preparing a commentary on the lectionary readings for several weeks in advance and found himself riveted by the ancient prophetic words.

How long, O Lord? I cry for help
    but you do not listen!
I cry out to you, "Violence!"
    but you do not intervene.
Why do you let me see ruin;
    why must I look at misery?
Destruction and violence are before me;
    there is strife and clamorous discord.
Then the Lord answered me and said:
    Write down the vision
Clearly upon the tablets,
    so that one can read it readily.
For the vision still has its time,
    presses on to fulfillment, and will not disappoint;
If it delays, wait for it,
    it will surely come, it will not be late. [Habakkuk 1:2–3; 2:2–3]

For Everything Its Season

As I lived with this passage over the next days, its many layers began to unfold themselves. What I heard first was a reassurance—that indeed the promises of God that spring from the deepest longings of our hearts and have been preached, sung, ritually enacted, and lovingly considered by so many generations of faithful are, in fact, still trustworthy. Next I heard the cry, both mine and the author's and, by extension, all the cries of the nameless, forgotten mothers and fathers who have instinctively tried to construct a sacred canopy over their children yet whose reach has not been wide enough. In those words, I heard the anguish of families in New York, ruptured in the wake of the World Trade Center collapse, and the terror of thousands of Afghani women and children fleeing their homeland in paralyzing fear of a coming apocalypse. I heard the weeping of Palestinian and Israeli parents and the late-night moaning of the children of Ruwanda, Kosovo, Chechnya, and on and on and on.

Finally, I heard the Lord's reply to Habakkuk: *Write down the vision, write down the vision clearly upon the tablets so that one can read it readily.* And I heard that instruction as directed toward me, toward us, as well as toward the prophet twenty-five hundred years ago. Write it down. Speak it. Live it. The vision is of a God known to us as a deeply loving parent, one who knew us before we were carried in our mothers' wombs, who attends to us with such solicitude that the hairs on our heads are counted, who hides us in the shadow of sheltering wings, a God whose heart is pierced with love for us, who through the rush of blood and water brings us to new birth.

The vision is of ourselves, invited to love one another as we have been loved. Each of us with a new heart, a parental heart that has stretched so far that it loves enough to let go, not only of the adult children who have outgrown laps but of the small world that stays confined within four walls, on one street, in one neighborhood. A heart that can love enough and suffer enough to pray into despair so deeply that hope emerges on the other side. A heart that can dare to entrust what is dearest to the mystery of a world that still waits for the promises. A parent's heart ripened in its particular loving so fiercely that it can hear the cries of another's children as its own.

INVITATION TO REFLECTION

CHAPTER 1

1. Have you ever thought of yourself as having a vocation or a calling? Has parenthood or marriage ever seemed to be a "call" to respond more generously to the mystery and great questions of life?

2. Pay attention to the silence that underlies your busy family life. You might get up early on a Saturday morning before everyone is up and sit by the window with a cup of tea. Turn off the TV one spring evening and take a quiet walk in your neighborhood. Watch your children sleep. Step outside your back door one night and see the stars together. Or watch the sun rise.

3. Being a person of faith does not necessarily mean being a person who has all the answers. How has raising children invited you, willingly or not, into "living into the question"?

CHAPTER 2

1. Keep a log for one week. At the end of each day, record the ordinary moments that occurred earlier that connected you to the depth, width, height, and length of love.

2. "Desert places" are often places of encounter with our demons as well as with God. To what desert places are you led as a parent? What temptations do you find there? What do you learn about yourself?

3. Each day this week, spend time with a scripture passage that reminds you that you are a beloved child of God. Suggestions: Psalms 23, 131, 139; John 3:16, 1 John 3:1–2; Romans 8:14–17.

4. How do you make discernments in your family? Is the "sense of spirit" or prayer a guiding principle? If not, how might it be?

CHAPTER 3

1. Take some time together as a family. What are the specific "sacred spaces" in your experience where you sense the "more" of your life together? What happens in those spaces? Do you have special rituals that occur there? How do you feel when you inhabit or remember these sacred spots?

2. How has living with others in family taught you something about God or the way God might love?

CHAPTER 4

1. Our stories point to the values we celebrate together. How does that story reflect the values that your family shares?

2. Spend time together going through old photo albums, either those of your immediate or your extended family. What do they say to you? You might want to focus on the photos that link the larger story of faith to your smaller family story (for example, baptisms, weddings, funerals).

3. What part of the wider culture's commercial narrative threatens the deeper values your family holds? Discuss ways you might resist that commercial story or ways you might create an alternative narrative for your family.

4. You might take a contemplative walk through your home or a home in which you once lived for some time either by yourself or with family members. Tell yourself the story of the people who inhabited this space and the things that happened in the rooms of the house.

CHAPTER 5

1. What are the various unnecessary demands that claim your attention and keep you from being truly available to family members? How might you let these things go or diminish their claims on you?

2. Bring to mind several family "snapshot" moments that invited you into the radical risk of genuinely loving another person.

3. How do you or might you and your family consciously honor Sabbath times of rest and rejuvenation?

4. How has this "fleshy, finite world" been a privileged place of encounter with God for you?

CHAPTER 6

1. What places do you call home? Why?

2. How has the natural environment in which you live shaped your sense of the holy?

3. Take a long, leisurely walk in your neighborhood. Pay attention to both the "habitude" and the "habitat" in which you dwell. Savor it. Reflect on the ways you have been shaped by the neighborhood's people and ethos, as well as by the weather, terrain, and landscape.

4. Keep a year-long journal of the various flowers, trees, and plants that you discover in your neighborhood walks.

CHAPTER 7

1. What rituals from your faith tradition have given shape to your family's spiritual life? How have these rituals created identity and community?

2. What are the unique rituals that your family practices—those patterned behaviors that make you who you are? Food rituals? Holiday rituals? Vacation rituals? Claim them and be grateful.

INVITATION TO REFLECTION

3. What are the "sacred sites" that family members feel drawn to? How has the sense of the sacred developed there over time?

CHAPTER 8

1. If welcoming and letting go might be said to be the twin arts of family spirituality, how have you practiced these arts?

2. Write the names of each of your children and grandchildren. Next to each of them, list the ways that child has "formed" you. What do you learn about yourself, your gifts, your weaknesses? How has love slowly grown in you with each child?

3. What "new grace" is available to you today?

4. Has parenting or family life ushered you into any experience you might term a "dark night"? How were you, or might you, be "repatterned" in the darkness?

CHAPTER 9

1. Have a family meeting to discuss the ways in which you live, or might live, the countercultural arts of the Christian life.

2. The struggle to meet the often-conflicting demands of social conscience and family responsibility are very real. Recall times when you feel you have successfully achieved this balance. When have you felt an imbalance? How might balance be found?

3. Each day for two weeks, pray with one of the traditional spiritual and corporal works of mercy. At the end of the two weeks, observe which of your reflections resurfaces. Pray for another two weeks with the work of mercy that might be realized in your family or by your family.

INVITATION TO REFLECTION

CHAPTER 10

1. Practice disarming gestures—the family hug, the listening ear—with members of your family.

2. If you are bound by the inability to forgive or if you hold another bound, bring it to the person or persons who are your spiritual support. With their help, explore ways you might unbind yourself and others.

3. Reconciliation requires that we first experience ourselves as treasured and cherished; only then can we see each other through eyes of love. Recall a time when you knew yourself as treasured either by God or by another. Bring this memory to any needed healing of your family in the present.

CHAPTER 11

1. How have the layers of meaning inherent in each liturgical season (Advent, Christmas, Lent, Easter, Ordinary time) built up over the years as your family has grown?

2. Calling to mind your children and parents, practice holding your hands shut tight and then opening them. Imagine what it is you find yourself holding onto, then imagine the new gifts with which your wide-open hands might be filled.

3. Keep a family scrapbook for remembering. Use it to pray in gratitude. Allow yourself to move beyond nostalgia to the mystery of the present as it is and the gift of the entirety of your story.

4. In what ways do you experience the simple truth that "God meets me here"?

5. Draw a picture, choreograph a dance, or compose a poem of the patterns of your family that both express and give substance to its shared life.

6. Do your holidays have a "shadow side"? How might you move more deeply into that shadow to discover the beams of light there?

INVITATION TO REFLECTION

7. Tell a story of a family—your own or another—that has discovered a hope that rises out of the ashes of tragedy and despair.

8. What gifts of "spiritual tears" have you discovered in family life?

9. Take a walk in a garden, either your own or a public garden. In what ways is your faith evoked, shaped by, or linked to gardens?

10. Reflect on the truth that it is only a radical trust in God that enables us to let go.

NOTES

CHAPTER 1

The quote from Thomas Merton is in *The New Man* (Toronto-New York: Bantam Books, 1981), p. 36; the quote from Augustine of Hippo in *Confessions* is in book 10, chapter 6. On the definition of *contemplation,* see the classic work by Edward Cuthbert Butler, *Western Mysticism: The Teachings of SS Augustine, Gregory and Bernard on Contemplation and the Contemplative Life* (London: Constable, 1927). Jerome's invective is found in his "Against Helvidius: The Perpetual Virginity of Blessed Virgin Mary," in *Nicene and Post-Nicene Fathers of the Christian Church,* vol. 6: *St. Jerome: Letters and Select Works* (Grand Rapids, Mich.: Wm. B. Eerdmans, 1954), pp. 344–345. For an overview of the development of the sacramental theology of marriage within the tradition, consult Joseph Martos, *Doors to the Sacred: An Historical Introduction to Sacraments in the Catholic Church* (New York: Doubleday, 1981) and Michael G. Lawler, *Marriage and Sacrament: A Theology of Christian Marriage* (Collegeville, Minn.: Liturgical Press: A Michael Glazier Book, 1993). On family structure and Christian identity, see Michael G. Lawler and Gail S. Risch, "Covenant Generativity: Toward a Theology of Christian Family," *Horizons,* Spring 1999, *26*(1), p. 20. The latest English edition of *Br. Lawrence of the Resurrection* is *The Practice of the Presence of God,* a critical edition by Conrad De Meester, translated by Salvatore Sciurba, (Washington D.C.: ICS Publications, Institute of Carmelite Studies, 1994).

CHAPTER 2

Several fine contemporary treatments of discernment are available. See Debra K. Farrington, *Hearing with the Heart: A Gentle Guide for Discerning God's Will for Your Life* (San Francisco: Jossey-Bass, 2002) and Reuben Job, *A Guide to Spiritual Discernment* (Nashville: Upper Room Books, 1996). The Ignatian system (based on the insights of the sixteenth-century founder of the Jesuits, Ignatius Loyola) is described well by Joan Mueller, *Faithful Listening: Discernment in Everyday Life* (Kansas City: Sheed and Ward, 1996). Quaker communal arts of discernment are described by Howard H. Brinton, *Quaker Journals: Varieties of Religious Experience Among Friends* (Wallingford: Pendle Hill Publications, 1972). The San Juanist tradition of discernment is based on the teachings of the sixteenth-century Carmelite saint, John of the Cross. A remarkable contemporary rendering of John's perspective is by Constance Fitzgerald, "Impasse and Dark Night," in *Living with Apocalypse: Spiritual Resources for Social Compassion,* edited by Tilden Edwards (San Francisco: HarperCollins, 1984, pp. 93–116).

CHAPTER 3

I have quoted from Caryll Houselander, *The Reed of God,* reprint of the 8th edition (Westminster, Md.: Christian Classics, 1987), p. 65. She is a twentieth-century English spiritual writer.

CHAPTER 4

Different Christian denominations have been created over the question of how much of that original image and likeness as a human I actually retain, how much I can cooperate with divine love in restoring that lost image, whether my part consists simply in faith in a divine act of redemption or in some degree of participation in redemptive spiritual and corporal activity, and how much my redemption is dependent on participation in the ritual life of the community. On the importance of story, see Dan P. McAdams, *The Stories We Live By: Personal Myths and the Making of the Self* (New York: William Morrow, 1993), p. 11. On the question of families as communities of storytelling, I refer to Marjorie J. Thompson, *Family: The Forming Center* (Nashville, Tenn.: Upper Room Books, 1989), pp. 99–100. The Thomas Merton quote is from *The Asian Journal of Thomas Merton* (New York: New Directions Books, 1975), pp. 333–334.

CHAPTER 5

Francis de Sales' seventeenth-century classic *Introduction to the Devout Life,* translated by John K. Ryan (Garden City, N.Y.: Doubleday Image Books, 1972), p. 44, is cited here. The Christian practice of Sabbath keeping, understood as a day of rest from work, developed over the centuries. The earliest Christians distinguished themselves from their Jewish neighbors by celebrating the resurrection on the first rather than the seventh day of the week—a work day. In the fourth century, Sunday became a day for communal worship, but it was thirteen centuries before, in England, there was a convergence between the idea of Sabbath rest and worship on Sunday—the Lord's Day. For a contemporary Christian perspective on Sabbath, see Tilden Edwards, *Sabbath Time* (Nashville, Tenn.: Upper Room Books, 1992) and Dorothy Bass, *Receiving the Day: Christian Practices for Opening the Gift of Time* (San Francisco: Jossey-Bass, 2000). The deeply incarnational spiritual vision I refer to is expressed most clearly in Western Christian tradition in the periods of Christian humanist revival, especially in the sixteenth- and seventeenth-century Ignatian and Salesian traditions, which continue to explore these insights today. On this tradition, see especially my "The Ignatian/Salesian Imagination and Familied Life" in *The Holy Family in Art and Devotion,* edited by Joseph F. Chorpenning (Philadelphia: St. Joseph's University Press, 1998), pp. 104–109.

CHAPTER 6

The quotations on home are from Erazim Kohák, "Of Dwelling and Wayfaring," in *The Longing for Home,* edited by Leroy S. Rouner (Notre Dame, Ind.: University of Notre Dame Press, 1996), p. 45, and Karen J. Warren, "Ecofeminism and the Longing for Home," in the same volume, pp. 217–218. Gaston Bachelard is noted for his philosophy of space. See his *The Poetics of Space* (Boston: Beacon Press, 1959), pp. 4–5 and 91. The idea that home is a platform from which we interpret the present and envision the future is from Katherine Platt, "Places of Experience and the Experience of Place" in *Longing for Home,* edited by Leroy S. Rouner (University of Notre Dame Press, 1996), pp. 112–127. On habitude, consult John B. Jackson, *Discovering the Vernacular Landscape* (New Haven: Yale University Press), p. 91. Mountainman James Clyman is quoted in Merrill J. Mattes, *The Great Platte River Road: The Covered Wagon Mainline Via Fort Kearny to Fort Laramie* (Nebraska State Historical Society, 1969), p. 10. On the environment shaping our subjectivity, see Belden Lane's wonderful exploration of the spirituality of place in *The Solace of Fierce Landscapes: Exploring Desert and Mountain Spirituality* (New York: Oxford University Press, 1998), pp. 9–10. Lynn Schmidt's poem appears in *Cries of the Spirit: A Celebration of Women's Spirituality,* edited by Marilyn Sewell (Boston: Beacon Press, 1991), p. 255. Merton used the term "hidden ground of love" first in 1967 in an address at Smith College in Massachusetts. It appears later throughout his letters. See the collection edited by William H. Shannon, *The Hidden Ground of Love: The Letters of Thomas Merton on Religious Experience and Social Concern* (New York: Farrar, Straus & Giroux, 1985). I have used the phrase "the isness of things" in my *Sacred Dwelling: A Spirituality of Family Life* (Leavenworth, Kans.: Forest of Peace Books, 1994), p. 181ff. The Martin de Porres club was named for the Catholic mulatto saint from Peru who had a special sensitivity to the poor and marginalized.

CHAPTER 7

On the significance of ritual, see Tom F. Driver, *The Image of Ritual: Our Need for Liberating Rites that Transform Our Lives and Our Communities* (San Francisco: HarperSanFrancisco, 1991), p. 6.

CHAPTER 8

The quote from the early American saint and foundress of the parochial school system is found in a letter to Sr. Cecelia O'Conway, quoted in Josephine Burns, "Elizabeth Ann Seton and the Church," *Vincentian Heritage,* 1997, *18*(2), p. 197. And Elizabeth Seton doesn't only claim my attention because she's been deemed an official saint in the Roman tradition but because she raised four children as a widow, and two of them died in her arms. I make reference to my own essay "The Charism of Parenting" in *Retrieving Charisms for the Twenty-first Century,* edited by Doris Donnelly (Collegeville, Minn.: Liturgical Press, 1999), pp. 85–102. The essay was later published in altered form in *Family Ministry,* Spring 1999, *13*(1). In it, I list the capacity to welcome and let go, flexibility, discernment, empowerment, and reconciliation as the charisms or gifts of parenting. About the discussion of spiritual growth: although I do not conflate psychological and spiritual growth, the two are usually intertwined. Recent studies on types of intelligence by psychologists like Robert Emmons and Howard Gardner point to multiple forms of intelligence ranging from musical intelligence to interpersonal intelligence. See Robert A. Emmons, *The Psychology of Ultimate Concerns: Motivation and Spirituality in Personality* (New York: Guilford Press, 1999). The most insightful work on "dark nights" has been done by the late Quaker writer Sandra Cronk. See her *Dark Night Journey: Inward Re-Patterning Toward a Life Centered in God* (Wallingford, Penn.: Pendle Hill Publications, 1991), pp. 1, 41, and 46.

CHAPTER 9

Peter Maurin was the French peasant who cofounded the Catholic Worker. His "A Case for Utopia" is quoted in Dorothy Day, *Loaves and Fishes* (Maryknoll, N.Y.: Orbis Books, 1983), p. 27. It has been suggested that the traditional works of mercy are presently outmoded because if taken at face value they do not overtly address the problems of "structural sin" or seek to redress the root causes of societal ills. However, with proponents like Dorothy Day or the earlier Vincentian (St. Vincent de Paul) tradition—which includes the Missionaries, the Daughters of Charity, Elizabeth Ann Seton's Sisters of Charity, Catherine McCauley, foundress of the Sisters of Mercy—the performance of the works of mercy goes hand-in-hand with a vision of a reformed society based on Christian principals. See Robert Maloney, *The Way of Vincent de Paul: A Contemporary Spirituality in the Service of the Poor* (Brooklyn, N.Y.: New City Press, 1992) and Brigid O'Shea Merriman, *The Spirituality of Dorothy Day* (South Bend, Ind.: Notre Dame University Press, 2001). The scriptural roots of the works of mercy are Matthew 6:14, 18:15, and 25:35–41. Thomas Aquinas has perhaps the most systematic theological treatment of the works of mercy. The Sojourners Community Web site is http://www.sojourners.com. For an updated classic text on justice and family, see Kathleen and James McGinnis, *Parenting for Peace and Justice: Ten Years Later* (Maryknoll, N.Y.: Orbis Books, 1990).

CHAPTER 10

The Family Ministry Survey was conducted in 1984 by the National Association of Catholic Diocesan Family Life Ministers. On forgiveness, I cite Flora Slosson Wuellner's *Forgiveness, the Passionate Journey: Nine Steps to Forgiving Through Jesus' Beatitudes* (Nashville, Tenn.: Upper Room Books, 2001). On the domestic church, see Joann Heaney-Hunter, "Domestic Church: Guiding Beliefs and Daily Practices" and William P. Roberts, "The Family as Domestic Church: Contemporary Implications" in *Christian Marriage and Family: Con-*

186

NOTES

temporary Theological and Pastoral Perspectives, edited by Michael G. Lawler and William P. Roberts (Collegeville, Minn.: Liturgical Press, 1996), pp. 38–58 and 59–78.

CHAPTER 11

The text "Veni Veni Emmanuel" was composed in the ninth century; the translation is by John M. Neale (1818–1866). John M. C. Crum is the lyricist of "Now the Green Blade Rises." I quote Symeon the New Theologian, the Greek Orthodox medieval spiritual writer, *The Discourses,* translated by C. J. deCatanzaro (New York: Paulist Press, 1980), p. 31, and the Western medieval author Geoffroy of Vendôme, sermon 9, pp. 157–271, cited in *Dictionnaire de spiritualité ascetique et mystique,* vol. 9 (Paris: Beauchesne, 1937–1998), p. 298, as well as early monastic founder John Climacus, *The Ladder of Divine Ascent,* translated by Colm Luibheid and Norman Russell (New York: Paulist Press, 1982), pp. 127, 137, and 139, and fourteenth-century Italian holy woman Catherine of Siena, *The Dialogue,* translation and introduction by Suzanne Noffke (New York: Paulist Press, 1980), p. 170. A wonderful exploration of faith and imagination is Gerald J. Bednar's *Faith as Imagination: The Contribution of William F. Lynch* (Kansas City: Sheed and Ward, 1996). I cite page 101. *The Garden of the Soul: A Manual of Spiritual Exercises and Instructions for Christians Who, Living in the World, Aspire to Devotion* (Westminster, Md.: Newman Press, 1945) was written by Bishop Challoner; the first edition was published in 1740. Included in the text (among many practices) are morning and evening prayers, a formula for an examination of conscience, litanies, prayers, devotional practices such as the Way of the Cross, the Rosary, the Sacred Heart, Benediction, resolutions to serve God, and instructions for mental prayer. See my *Sacred Dwelling: A Spirituality of Family Life,* p. 34, for the quote about letting go. Some of the books on family spirituality that have sustained me over the years are Dolores Leckey, *The Ordinary Way: A Family Spirituality* (New York: Crossroad, 1982), Ernest Boyer Jr., *Finding God at Home: Family Life as Spiritual Discipline* (originally published as *A Way in the*

World (San Francisco: Harper & Row, 1988), Gertrude Mueller Nelson, *To Dance With God: Family Ritual and Community Celebration* (New York: Paulist Press, 1986), David M. Thomas, *Christian Marriage: A Journey Together* (Wilmington, Del: Michael Glazier, 1990), Anne Broyles, *Growing Together in Love: God Known Through Family Life* (Nashville: Upper Room Books, 1993), and Edward Hays, *Prayers for the Domestic Church: A Handbook for Worship in the Home* (Easton, Kans.: Forest of Peace Books, 1979). A more recent contribution has been Denise Roy, *My Monastery is a Minivan: Where the Daily is Divine and the Routine becomes Prayer* (Chicago: Loyola Press, 2001).

THE AUTHOR

Wendy M. Wright earned a Ph.D. from the University of California at Santa Barbara and is currently professor of theology and holds the John C. Kenefick Chair in the Humanities at Creighton University in Omaha, Nebraska. She also teaches regularly in several graduate ministerial programs and directs retreats. She is a frequent contributor to spiritual journals such as *Weavings* and the author of a number of books, including *Sacred Dwelling: A Spirituality of Family Life*. She and her husband, Roger Bergman, are the parents of three young adults.